6042753

CAREER SUCCESS / PERSONAL FAILURE

CAREER SUCCESS / PERSONAL FAILURE

ABRAHAM K. KORMAN, Ph.D.

Baruch College
City University of New York
BFS Psychological Associates

with RHODA W. KORMAN, M.S.

PRENTICE-HALL, INC., Englewood Cliffs, N.J. 07632

Library of Congress Cataloging in Publication Data

KORMAN, ABRAHAM K 1933-
   Career success, personal failure.

   Biliography: p.
   1. Executives—Psychology.   2. Alienation (Social psychology)   3. Success.   I. Korman, Rhoda W., joint author.   II. Title.
   HF5500.2.K67   658.4'09   80-10152
   ISBN 0-13-1114777-3

Editorial/production supervision
and interior design by Linda Stewart
Cover Design by Infield/D'Astolfo Associates
Manufacturing buyer: Harry P. Baisley

© 1980 by Prentice-Hall, Inc., Englewood Cliffs, N.J. 07632

All rights reserved. No part of this book
may be reproduced in any form or
by any means without permission in writing
from the publisher.

Printed in the United States of America

10 9 8 7 6 5 4 3 2 1

Prentice-Hall International, Inc., *London*
Prentice-Hall of Australia Pty. Limited, *Sydney*
Prentice-Hall of Canada, Ltd., *Toronto*
Prentice-Hall of India Private Limited, *New Delhi*
Prentice-Hall of Japan, Inc., *Tokyo*
Prentice-Hall of Southeast Asia Pte. Ltd., *Singapore*
Whitehall Books Limited, *Wellington, New Zealand*

To S & S
with Love

CONTENTS

AN OPENING STATEMENT   ix

MANAGEMENT ALIENATION:
    The Career Success/Personal
    Failure Syndrome   1

CAREER SUCCESS/PERSONAL FAILURE:
    The Management Experience
    An Analytic Framework   19

REDUCING CAREER SUCCESS/
PERSONAL FAILURE   71

SUMMARY   107

CASE STUDIES IN CAREER SUCCESS/
PERSONAL FAILURE   113

AN OPENING STATEMENT

The idea that personal satisfactions will result from career success has been with us a long time. It has played a major role in the formation of our society, the most economically successful society in history. We cannot discard this belief lightly, despite growing evidence that it is not universally true.

The problem of career success and personal failure is upon us and it is too serious in its implications for us to ignore. The consequences to the individual, our organizations, and to society are great if this problem is allowed to continue unchecked. We must address ourselves to determining why our most successful career people are showing such high degrees of personal and social alienation and why this distress seems to be growing. Appropriate correction mechanisms have to be found and implemented.

Most of the people we are writing about in this book are men in their midlife years although, clearly, there are women to whom much of what we say is applicable.

Women are beginning to advance within the world of work. Thus, while discussion of the career successful, personally alienated manager must today refer primarily to men, we may not be far away from the time when we will also discuss career success and personal failure in relation to women.

For the present, however, the term refers primarily to men and that is why we use masculine language in our discussion. Our use of male pronouns and phrases should, however, not be taken to mean that we wish to imply that women in the same situations do not experience similar problems. The small number of women who are presently successful high-level managers will recognize aspects of themselves. We feel certain, also, that regardless of the names in our studies or the pronouns we use, both men and women who are on their way to becoming managers might recoil from some of the pictures we paint of the men who currently hold the positions at which they are aiming. Let them all be warned that what is happening to men in midlife today can just as easily be fated for them, regardless of sex, unless we begin to cope with the personal alienation implicit in our modern version of career success.

If this book can move us at least a small step along the road, it will serve its purpose well.

ACKNOWLEDGEMENTS

The completion of a book is a time of joy and a time of relief. The task is finally over. With these feelings comes also the recognition that there are other contributors to a book besides the authors. Such is the case here. We would like to take this opportunity to thank the following individuals for their contributions to this book: Ms. Barbara Piercecchi, Management Acquisitions Editor for Prentice-Hall for her suggestions; Ms. Linda Stewart, our Production Editor, for the arduous task of putting it all together into one piece; and Profs. Robert Guest of Dartmouth College, Jerome Schnee of Rutgers University and Richard Ritti of Pennsylvania State University for their valuable commnts on an earlier version of the manuscript. All have contributed greatly to the development of his book.

CAREER SUCCESS / PERSONAL FAILURE

MANAGEMENT ALIENATION:

The Career Success/Personal Failure Syndrome

At age 45, Frank Brown is a self-made man. Although he has no academic degrees or special training, Brown was recently promoted to the vice presidency of a medium-sized manufacturing company. He is known as an assertive man who makes friends easily and is very active in community affairs (secretary of his lodge, president of his church group, Citizen of the Year in his town). He is married, has a son who was recently married and a daughter in college.

Despite many physical complaints, Brown is in good condition, other than being slightly overweight. His complaints include "gall bladder" attacks (no physiological basis was found for these), "allergic" irritation of the eyes, lower back pain, and insomnia. He was referred to a psychiatrist after his intestinal discomforts were unrelieved by medical treatment.

Critical History

After being discharged from the Army, Brown obtained a supervisory position in a large West Coast city. He married soon after and was sent to a branch office in the Midwest. He worked his way through staff positions and was eventually asked to set up an office in another city.

The family relocated and their first child was born. After spending five years in the new city, Brown accepted a more lucrative job, and the family moved again. He remained in this position for several years, having little difficulty in organizing and running a small office while he and his wife became involved in community activities and extensive entertaining. A second child was born.

Brown then accepted a job organizing an office for a new company, and his business responsibilities increased to include the hiring of staff and the supervision of middle-management personnel. He had little contact with lower-echelon personnel in the organization thereafter, but was well liked by the "management team." It was during this period that Mrs. Brown developed a number of psychosomatic complaints and the children began to manifest behavioral disorders necessitating referral to a child-guidance clinic.

The growth of the corporation resulted in management moving to another city. Mrs. Brown resented this move, but accepted it. After several years Brown began to feel that his outside activities were somehow not pleasing; he no longer looked forward to lodge and church meetings. His wife became active in various organizations, but the couple had few activities in common other than those involving Brown's business associates.

As his responsibility grew, Brown found that he had to spend increasing amounts of time "checking" his subordinates and ensuring the smooth operation of his branch of the organization. His social life began to be restricted to business contacts, and even his occasional golf games were with people he knew in the business world. He became briefly depressed, but he was not aware of predominantly feeling this emotion.

Mrs. Brown suffered a more severe depression, consulted several psychiatrists, and began to take tranquilizing and antidepressant medication. The couple's sexual life dwindled and eventually stopped. It was during this time that Brown was referred to the psychiatrist. In addition to his physical problems, he complained that his wife did not understand him and had little sympathy for his discomfort. He also felt that he could no longer communicate with his children.

Now, at times of business expansion and business activity, Brown's depression is relieved and he is unaware of any difficulties. His physical complaints remain, however, and his secretary has taken the role of "nurse." The marital adjustment of his son has not been good, his daughter has been involved in numerous antisocial and rebellious activities, and his wife has become a regular psychiatric patient.

Source: J. Steiner, What price success? *Harvard Business Review,* March–April 1972, 50 (2), 69–74.

The case of Frank Brown is not unusual today. He is typical of an increasing number of managers and executives who are reporting (1) great dissatisfaction with life, (2) strong feelings of personal and social alienation, and, frequently, (3) a desire to give up the position in life which they have worked hard to achieve and which defines them as successful. If this trend continues, the result will be a progressive decay of our institutions and organizations. This deterioration, if unchecked, has calamitous implications for the individuals who work for these organizations and also for our society, which depends for its viability on the health of these same institutions and the people who run them.

We have assumed for a long time that the managers who run our organizations are more committed to them than are people who are not as successful. We have also assumed that they are more satisfied in other, non-job-related aspects of their lives, partly as a result of their career success. Managers have been thought to be more motivated to work and more job-satisfied than others in the work organization because their job success translates into a high social position in their business and private lives. We see them as more reliable in carrying out organizational duties and as more characterized by creative, higher-level achievement needs than those at lower levels within the organization.

It is now becoming apparent that these assumptions are increasingly less valid and that managers are becoming more negative in their overall job perspectives. The significance of this is that because managers can exert great discretionary power in their work activities and are also prominent in the organization, and because they are directly free to implement whatever positive or negative attitudes they have, their negative behaviors are potentially damaging to the functioning of the system.

Since what managers do is highly visible, they may affect other people in the organization by serving as role models for them. If their attitudes and behaviors are good, fine. But if they are behaving negatively, those activities which are detrimental may be judged appropriate and emulated by those lower in the organization. Moreover, these same negative behaviors may serve to change the aspirations of those who may have been thinking of management as a career.

When they are functioning poorly, managers in both the public and private sectors also affect the general functioning of our society in other ways. Behaviorally, attitudinally, and philosophically, we have always been a society that promised great personal satisfaction for success based on materialistic acquisition and/or competitive supremacy. Alienation and negative attitudes among the successful (e.g., managers) is, therefore, unexpected, and these unconfirmed expectancies can be great sources of discontent.

Problems of family life and work experience, when they crop up among the successful, may make the individual involved feel guilty, while causing disquiet and doubt among onlookers. According to our cultural mythology, such successful people should be happy. But they may not be. This makes them feel even worse, raising the level of individual negative emotion and causing such people to view life increasingly as a negative experience. Since the educational and governmental institutions that have supported this mythology eventually come to be viewed in a more pessimistic light as part of this overall pattern, there is a loss in the support which these institutions can expect from these unhappy people. Since society has traditionally looked for leadership to the successful person who is high on the socioeconomic scale, this creates a loss in the viability of its institutions. It becomes increasingly unlikely that they will be able to call upon these disillusioned people in the future, thus ensuring an accelerating downhill trend.

How bad is the situation? Do all managers show these negative attitudes? Not at all. We need to stress that many managers, probably most, do have satisfying, meaningful lives. Research studies have also shown that managers, on the average, like their jobs more than do people lower in the organization.[1] However, it has become apparent that an increasing number of people are reporting substantial life dissatisfaction. Consider the following statements, each based on recent independent research studies:

  1. Individuals with high levels of income did not report any greater satisfaction with life in a practical sense

than did individuals with lower levels of income. This is true when we look at the United States as a whole (using systematic random sampling) and when we repeat the research in a smaller, more narrowly defined metropolitan area.[2,3] (These findings are among the most illustrative of those changes in our society which are of major interest to us in this book.)

2. Highly successful male executives in midlife reported doubts about the meaning of success, considerable self-doubt, disquiet over their careers (despite their success), and great value conflict.[4]

3. A lack of personal fulfillment and a sense of job meaninglessness was found to be common among both higher- and lower-level executives in a highly profitable corporation with a good employment history.[5]

4. A survey of several thousand managers who attended courses run by a well-known training association reported great degrees of personal alienation (i.e., their careers were no longer meeting their needs) and, also, alienation from the organizations for which they worked.[6]

5. Intensive interviews of successful young executives and their wives revealed great feelings of stress, a loss of personal alertness, and an increasing sense of meaninglessness in everyday activities.[7]

6. Significant numbers of successful managers in today's corporations reported a loss of emotional feeling and a decreased level of social and emotional ties with others.[8]

7. A survey of one thousand middle-aged professionals and managers found that approximately 80% went through periods of intense frustration as early as their late 30s, and that 15% never fully recovered from this period.[9]

8. The belief that people higher in an organization are more involved in their jobs than those lower in the organization has not been supported by research evidence.[10]

These data supply the evidence for our viewpoint. They document the fact that the problem exists and, to some degree, tell us about its extensiveness. They do not tell us, however, about the emotional characteristics of this problem and the concrete, specific ways in which it becomes manifested. Such a description is provided in Table 1, in which we present a series of concrete recollections and graphic descriptions of "what it is like" or "what it was like" by working managers who have reported on the nature of their experiences.

TABLE ONE
Illustrations of Management Alienation

"I'd never had any great goals for myself as a high-level executive. When I was with _____ I realized that I'd rather have time off than a raise. I wanted to start at $10,000 a year for five days' work, and after five years be getting $10,000 a year for three days' work.

"But they made it clear to me that there wasn't room at _____ for anyone who felt that way. The corporate pipelines need people who can be promoted and if you don't consider working longer hours, giving up more of your private life, and moving up to more things you can't afford as 'getting ahead,' a corporation doesn't have space for you on the treadmill. You have to get off so someone else can have your place."

(page 63)

"Organizations oppress you. .....They hold you down. I felt as if industry were consuming me. It took what it wanted, but didn't put anything back. It doesn't allow one to grow as a person. You can grow in its image, but that's the only way. I don't admire the guy who's president of a company any more. In fact, I feel pretty sorry for him."

(page 8)

"When I could no longer take the company I was working for, I was fortunate to have something that was really powerful and positive and demanding that I could say 'yes' to. I think the problem for most men who want to get out is not making a living—they can find a way to do that. It's that they've lost touch with their *feelings* about what's right for them. You can't live with the demands of the corporation without turning off your feelings to some extent, so you can't sense your gut reactions to things as well, can't tell what's right for you. I don't know how to solve that one."

(page 50)

Source: D. Biggs, *Breaking Out* (New York: David McKay Company, Inc., 1973).

"I asked Charlie if he saw heavy financial responsibilities as one of the major pressures causing divorce among people our age. He said he did a lot of divorce work and: 'There's no doubt in my mind that at some point in every sensitive man's life he says, why am I doing this? He compares his youthful expectations with his middle-aged status and thinks do I want to do this for twenty more years, and he says hell no I don't. And that applies to everything. I think a lot of that is more vocational than domestic. I've used the term *selling widgets*. After you've sold widgets for twenty-five years, and are the best widget seller in the country, then the very thought of selling another widget is abhorrent. This causes a terrible questioning and is a shaking and shattering experience that goes through all your relationships, including family. Particularly if you are under heavy financial burdens. People tend to think of themselves as trapped in the position of producing large sums of money that get gobbled up by other people. They feel sorry for themselves. Of course, everybody has the same problem.'"

(page 124)

"Then Charlie turned back to what he had been saying earlier. 'Somehow our society is such that life for men ends at age twenty-five. By that time you're supposed to be educated and you're supposed to be married and you're supposed to be in your job. And we're all brought up to believe that things as they are at twenty-five are the way they're supposed to be for the rest of our lives. And that's just not right. A change in careers ought to be the expected, rather than the aberrant. So that when a guy has practiced law for twenty-five years and gotten to be pretty good at it, then he would do something else. Two or three careers in a man's lifetime. Because spending forty years doing the same kind of work is stultifying. It's burdensome and it tends to limit horizons to a very great degree.'"

(page 125)

"He paused, then went on: 'The American dream is to have a nice house and two nice cars and some nice children. When you get there, when you've got all those things, you find out they just aren't worth a damn. They're fine, but as far as being the significance of your life, they're vastly and woefully inadequate. And yet, when we get to that point, we don't know what to do. Nobody's ever told us, nobody's ever—you know, every man thinks his own experience is unique. Maybe we ought to have a male menopause anonymous society or something. Then when you'—he laughed—'feel like life has passed you by, you can find out everybody else feels that way too.'"

(page 125)

"He said he sure had. 'You know, by the time you're middle-aged and you've worked this long, you know how it works. You know how people are motivated and you know how in many ways it's a grubby, sordid, unidealistic existence. Just about everybody's materialistic and self-centered. I worried about it because I knew I was raising my children with ideas that weren't necessarily going to help them get along in this kind of country—like being idealistic or socially motivated. I knew what it took to survive in this society, and the attitudes I had given them were not the right ones for that.' Lord. What a devastating admission: a man gives to his sons the ideals he most deeply believes in, and then fears he has handicapped them, I mentioned this to John."

(page 77)

"We were, most of us, good little boys, good scouts, game players, determinedly heterosexual suitors, and dutifully monogamous husbands. We fought the largest of wars, GI Joes, and after that: a silent generation, not to be trusted because we were over thirty, the power structure; racists, if white (though we might protest not so), inferior, if black (though the opposite might be demonstrable), and chauvinist pigs, all. At the same time, good husbands, proud fathers, grimly enduring the rat race, men in gray flannel suits, organization men, and paying the bills, buying the split-levels, paying the taxes that each year made us dread the beautiful onset of spring, buying the insurance that made us worth more dead than alive, attending the PTA, boosting the Little League, footing the college bills, paying the alimony and child support—and ever the dutiful sons, seeing after sick and enfeebled parents, guilt-haunted when we had to put them in nursing homes."

(page 56)

"The jobless men I met did not talk about these things, but I wondered how many of them were fed up with being abstractions—chauvinist, bill payer, dear old Dad. Every other element in society has risen up and thrown off some yoke of abstraction—blacks, women, youth. But not *the man.* All we have done was what was expected of us in all those abstract roles. Blacks and whites of us, we kept things going while the black movement won its victories. Women and youth could not have mounted their movements if we had not been going to work and paying the bills. When, I asked myself, would it be our turn to be heard, we who are supposed to belong to the most powerful group in the land?"

(page 56)

Source: P. Watters, *The Angry Middle-Aged Man* (New York: Grossman Publishers, 1976).
An Analytic Framework

This book will focus first on the factors that seem to be generating career success and personal failure, particularly among managers and executives. What is society's contribution? What stems from organizational life itself? What is the influence, if any, of the aging process? How does growing older affect feelings of personal failure among those who have had successful careers? Although some feelings of failure among successful career people may well be inevitable, much can be done to reduce the dysfunctional effects of alienation on society, organizations, and individuals. Therefore, we will also examine some of these methods, approaches, and techniques and see how they can be appropriately utilized.

SOME CLARIFICATION OF TERMS AND DEFINITIONS

Until now we have been using *career success, alienation,* and *satisfaction/dissatisfaction* in their everyday, layman sense. We now need to define these terms more specifically and concretely before we use them in our analysis of the career success/personal failure syndrome among managers.

What is success? What do we mean when we describe managers as having achieved career success? Success means the materialistic, status-oriented, power-over-others factors that we have long accepted as defining "I made it." Occupational sociologists have almost always found that income, power over others, and uniqueness tend to be most crucial in the ranking of occupational status in this country, with particular emphasis on income and power. Although not all managers rank high on both of these, most rank fairly high and many are very high. Furthermore, it has been the traditional formal logic of organizations to consider the manager to be a successful person. Most people enter the organization with the image of the manager as defining success for that system, even if they come into the system as technical specialists. After all, it is management that runs the organization; managers are the bosses. It is not surprising, then, that managers and executives generally rank high in occupational status studies.

Suppose the manager does not consider himself to be a career success? What does it matter if sociological studies show him to be in one of the higher occupations? Although this is certainly possible, we would propose that (1) this feeling is less likely to occur at the top end of the hierarchy than at the lower end, and (2) the manager would still have the knowledge that at least other people consider him to be a career success, even if he believes otherwise. Such a feeling of social approval is not shared by the factory assembly-line worker.

Are we moving away from this traditional definition of success? We think so, but slowly. One reason is that we have assumed that career success is necessary and desirable for personal success, an assumption we are now finding increasingly false. However, most individuals still subscribe to our traditional norms, even though it is apparent that we now need to change our perspectives on what we mean by success.

While success, however defined, is basically positive, dissatisfaction and alienation are *different* types of negative feelings with complex interrelationships. They are *not* the same. *Job dissatisfaction* is the extent to which the individual views his job as unpleasant and a source of negative emotion. "I don't like it" expresses his feelings.

While job satisfaction involves an evaluation of one's job, the key emotion underlying alienation is a sense of separation or estrangement. Two types of alienation concern us in this book: personal alienation and social alienation. The first involves seeing oneself as behaving in a manner that does not match one's image of oneself as one is. It is having the belief that there is a "real self" inside the individual who is not getting a chance to express himself. The surface person, the one who is behaving in the world everyday, is not that real person. There is a split, a separation, or, if you will, a sense of personal alienation.

Consider the case of Manager A, who thinks well of himself. As a result, his personal needs are so important to him that he desires to have them met by his job situation. When they are not, he is dissatisfied. We call this type of individual *non-alienated* since (1) he is aware of what his personal needs are; (2) he desires to have his needs satisfied by his job; and (3) he is unhappy when these needs are not being met. He is, therefore, a nonalienated person who can be either satisfied or dissatisfied with his job, depending on his level of need satisfaction. Alienation and satisfaction (or dissatisfaction) are not the same.

Similarly, consider Manager B, who does not think much of himself. Since his personal needs belong to him and he is not worth much, he has little regard for his needs and does not, therefore, evaluate his job based on whether or not his needs have been met. As a result, he is as likely to consider himself satisfied when his needs have not been met as when they have been met. We would call such an individual *personally alienated,* since he is out of touch with himself in that he does not use his own interests and needs in making his behavioral choices and evaluating his satisfaction with his job. If he is satisfied with his job, this may be as a result of such factors as whether the job meets social standards or the desires of one's friends or family. Here, also, we see that alienation is not the same as satisfaction; one can be personally alienated and still be satisfied or dissatisfied.

Independent of this feeling, there is an attitude we call social alienation. This is seeing oneself as being split, or separated, from the people around one. There are no grounds on which to meet if one is socially alienated from others and has no common framework upon which to interact with them. One is alone in the truest sense of the word.

In this book our major focus is on alienation, both personal and social. We are interested in how the individual feels about himself and the conditions of his life, rather than in how he evaluates his job. In effect, we are defining personal failure as being composed primarily of a sense of personal and social alienation.

> The detachment of worker from his work is similar to the detachment in the schizoid condition described by R. D. Laing. The individual who is subjected to the stress of "a threatening experience from which there is no physical escape" develops an elaborate protective mechanism; "he becomes a mental observer, who looks on, detached and impassive at what his body is doing or what is being done to his body." For that person, "the world is a prison without bars, a concentration camp without barbed wire." Instead of experiencing reality directly, he develops a "false" self as a buffer for the real world, while the real self retires to an "inner" position of unexposed safety. All of life seems full of "futility, meaninglessness, and purposelessness," since it is not, in fact, being directly experienced. The real self is completely blocked, barred from any spontaneous expression or real freedom of action and totally sterile. In the absence of a spontaneous natural, creative relationship with the world which is free from anxiety, the "inner self" thus develops an overall sense of inner impoverishment, which is experienced in complaints of the emptiness, deadness, coldness, dryness, impotence, desolation, worthlessness, of the inner life.
>
> *Source:* Excerpt from *Job Power* by David Jenkins, copyright © 1973 by David Jenkins; reprinted by permission of Doubleday & Company, Inc., p. 43.

Detachment is an experience that destroys human beings and the social context in which they live. It generates seeking and accepting negative outcomes for the self. After all, life is not real for detached people. The real self is dying anyway. Being alienated also generates doing negative things to others. After all, it is not the real self that is doing these things but somebody with the same name who is doing his job, however dirty it may be.

This description of alienation and its implications is, however, basically emotional. We can be more analytic and specific as to why alienation, personal and social, is bad for individuals, organizations, and society and why it is important that we try to reduce it as much as possible through appropriate organizational and societal intervention programs.

Consider, for a moment, a person who feels himself personally and socially alienated and who does not see any possibility for change. His perception of himself is that of an individual who is not meeting his personal needs and whose real self is not being expressed in his everyday behavior. His perception of others shows an analogous pattern, in that he views his interactions with them as unreal, since it is not his real self who is interacting with them. It is somebody else with his name. His real self is inside, not being expressed and, maybe, dying. As a result, he also feels a sense of social alienation from others. How do these feelings translate into behavior? This can occur in a number of ways.

Since one technique for reducing a sense of disquiet and negative feelings is to try to see only those people who are like ourselves so that it will not seem as bad as if we were there alone, the alienated person, who we will assume is an organizational manager, might become highly antagonistic to individuals who are not like him. Among the kinds of people to whom this alienated individual might become particularly hostile are (1) creative people who are willing to challenge the norms of his work organization and who are capable of initiating some desirable innovation; (2) younger people coming into his work organization who are not necessarily creative but who express in no uncertain terms that they will not allow the organization to generate a sense of personal and/or social alienation in them; and (3) any individuals (young, old, male, female, white, black, etc.) who indicate to him that there is another set of experiences possible in life and within organizations than the kind of experiences which this alienated individual is having.

Nothing would matter to the alienated manager; his only interest would be to surround himself with people like himself in order to allay his misery. Anybody symbolizing anything different would be a threat to him because the experience of such a person implies that he does not have to be as alienated as he is since others are not. (Maybe, therefore, his alienation is his fault.) Hence, these different kinds of people are to be resisted, even at the risk of precipitating interorganizational conflict and keeping out individuals who might make a contribution.

Change programs designed to reduce alienation would suffer similarly. The individual who is alienated and sees no possibility of change for himself would resist these programs to the greatest degree possible because of his fear that they may succeed in decreasing the number of people in the organization who are like him. There are two ways in which he might show his resistance. First, he might attempt to stop the programs entirely. This is not always possible, however. As an alternative, he might try to neutralize the effects of these programs. One way of doing this would be to bureaucratize them by making them conform to the same procedures and organizational demands that led to his (and others') alienation in the first place. Another way would be to develop and structure organizational staffs that would fight alienation only in the manner in which he would approve. The growth of staffs developed in this manner would mean that (1) the alienation would not be reduced and (2) more individuals would support him in fighting alienation in the way he desires because more people would have their jobs at stake in using the particular techniques recommended by the alienated manager. In other words, the more such staffs are developed, the more we have organizational resources devoted to resolving a problem in a manner that guarantees nonsuccess. Furthermore, the situation might become worse over time as these procedures become traditional and legitimatized and the likelihood of adopting alternative techniques for reducing alienation decreases.

The alienated manager is also a problem in other ways. In the interest of reducing his negative perceptions of himself and his life, he may view other people as not being any different than he is. He can then ignore the needs and values of others since (1) they are no different than he is and he knows himself, and (2) he ignores his own needs so why shouldn't he ignore the needs of others? Why should he pay more attention to others than he does to himself? He cannot and does not, with the result that this increases his social alienation while reducing his ability to manage others and to integrate them into a cohesive work unit. His behavior is marked by an unresponsiveness to individuality in general, a disparaging of specific idiosyncratic characteristics even if they are organizationally useful, and an inability to relate to subordinates on any meaningful personal level, including the simplest task-oriented way. Instead, the alienated manager demands a blind, uncritical acceptance of the policies and practices that generated his own alienation.

The alienated manager may act in the same manner when dealing with other work units besides his own and when dealing with clients or customers. In both cases, he shows a lack of concern for the legitimate needs and desires of other individuals and groups, an acceptance of unthinking, uncaring service toward them, and an anger should they react negatively to his treatment of their wishes. After all, how dare they call him to task for ignoring their needs? He doesn't protest to those in the organization who ignore his needs!

This is not only theory. There is research evidence that shows that these self- and organizationally defeating acts actually do occur. Each of the following statements is based on the findings of an empirical research study and, when taken together, support what we have been describing.

1. People whose jobs reflect their personal interests show increasing mental health with job experience.[11]

2. People who feel a sense of external control* (or powerlessness) are more likely to be more passive in their political behavior and perform more poorly on the job.[11,12]
3. People who feel a sense of disconfirmed expectancies on their jobs and a sense of contradictory role demands* are more likely to perform poorly on their jobs.[13]
4. Individuals who are personally alienated and not using their personal needs as bases for choice are less achieving, less creative, and more hostile.[14]
5. People who show personal alienation are more prone to mental disorder, suicide, and a low level of information about life.[15]
6. Individuals who exhibit cultural estrangement and social isolation from others are more likely to show ethnic prejudice, mental disorder, and suicide.[16]

Alienation, obviously a very negative emotional state for an individual, has a definite effect on his or her behavior. An individual who has been career-motivated and integrated in a personal and social sense, may lose this guiding focus and have nothing with which to replace it. Without such a restructuring, these changes can become detrimental to him personally, to his employing organization, and to society.

Alienation must, therefore, be distinguished from job satisfaction, which is a more ambiguous concept. Job satisfaction, on the one hand, often describes the feelings of a healthy, striving individual who demands and obtains personal need satisfaction at work. In the course of obtaining this satisfaction, he will often seek goals that will put his striving in concordance with the needs of the organization. However, job satisfaction can also describe the feelings of a withdrawn, apathetic person who wants, expects, and obtains little from his work and does little in return. The first is a good situation for all concerned and the second is not. Yet,

---

*These conceptual ideas will be expanded further later in the text as major sources of management alienation.

both individuals might have high job satisfaction. Similarly, a low-satisfaction, nonalienated individual who is striving to find a more meaningful job is not the same as a nonsatisfied, alienated person who doesn't care.

It is for these reasons that alienation, both personal and social, is the major focus of this book. However, we will refer to the job satisfaction of managers, when appropriate, and also to the related ideas of career and life satisfaction. Both of these latter attitudes are similar to the job satisfaction concept, in that they each involve an evaluation of a specific external experience (i.e., career and life). Unfortunately, these concepts are subject to the same ambiguity of interpretation as that related to job satisfaction.

Closely akin to the concepts of alienation and satisfaction is *loss of work interest*. Loss of work interest can reflect a particular type of social alienation for some managers. Managers and executives are often people who have been highly work oriented in the past. If they had not been, they would not have risen to their present prominence. To lose a feeling of work commitment may be a particularly strong type of alienation for these people, since this loss is a loss of a part of themselves that was once highly important to them, i.e. their work commitment.

THE MANAGEMENT EXPERIENCE

An Analytic Framework

AN OVERALL VIEW

The psychodynamics of business and family life interacting with the realities of the midlife aging process appear to be the major factors leading to the personal and social alienation seen among successful, middle-aged managers. These factors are illustrated in Figure 1.

At a certain point in life, generally starting in the mid-30s, a cognitive awareness of contradictory life demands emerges. Expectancies have not always been fulfilled and with maturity has come the knowledge that hoped-for goals and/or rewards will probably never be achieved. There is a sense of having been controlled by the outside world—the corporation's structure, family needs, social obligations. Affiliative satisfactions are now also hard to come by, because somewhere along the way old friends and coworkers have been shed, wives have become liberated and, often, estranged, and children have grown into strangers whose college tuition must be paid, but who bring little joy and companionship into the household. Social interactions of a noncareer nature may also have become routinized and, as often happens, primarily of a business-related nature, whether by design or the accident of success.

At the same time, age is advancing rapidly. The manager is aware of younger, bright, dynamic men, with their illusions still intact, coming up behind him.

The feelings of personal and social alienation resulting from these pressures may be enormous. There is a loss of interest in the very activities that have sustained the manager during most of his adulthood. He cares less about his job or work or the organization that employs him. His family life is painful and his social life gives no surcease from his agony.

This is a grim picture of psychological distress. But it is possible for growth to occur. A desire for a rearticulation of one's life perspectives and purposes may emerge. It is at this point that the work organization can intervene with appropriate programs. Or the executive can look to resources in the community that will enable him to examine his life in a flexible manner and make decisions about changing those aspects of life that cause him the most unhappiness.

FIGURE 1

Model of Career Success and Personal Failure

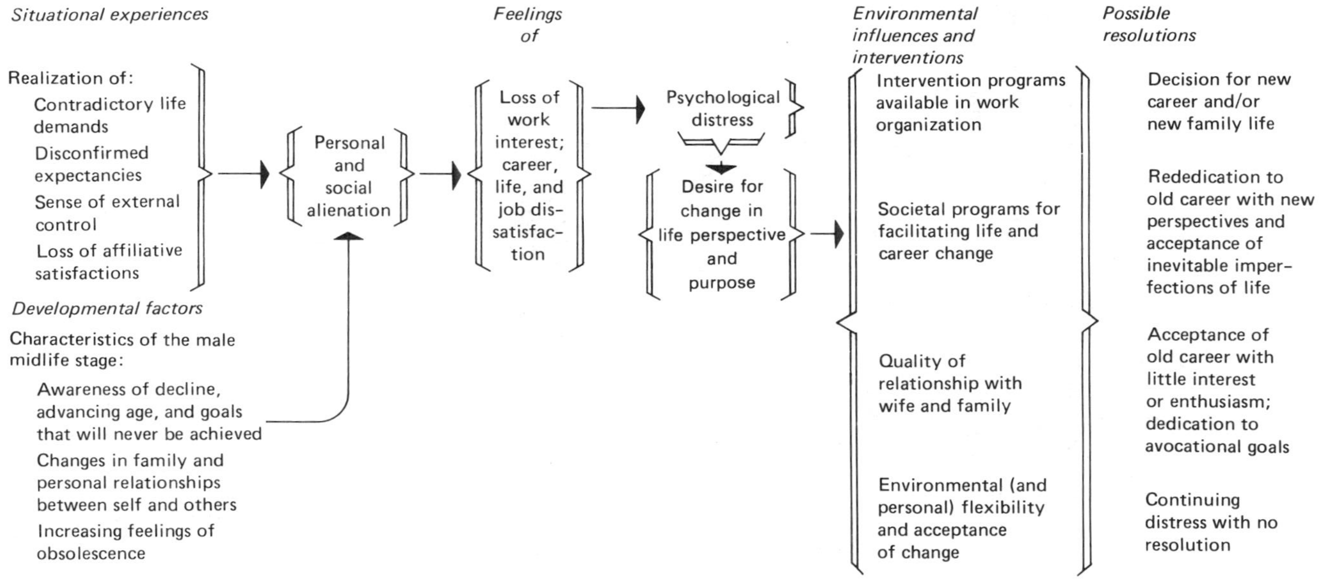

Situational experiences

Realization of:
Contradictory life demands
Disconfirmed expectancies
Sense of external control
Loss of affiliative satisfactions

Developmental factors

Characteristics of the male midlife stage:
Awareness of decline, advancing age, and goals that will never be achieved
Changes in family and personal relationships between self and others
Increasing feelings of obsolescence

→ Personal and social alienation →

Feelings of

Loss of work interest; career, life, and job dissatisfaction

→ Psychological distress

→ Desire for change in life perspective and purpose

Environmental influences and interventions

Intervention programs available in work organization

Societal programs for facilitating life and career change

Quality of relationship with wife and family

Environmental (and personal) flexibility and acceptance of change

Possible resolutions

Decision for new career and/or new family life

Rededication to old career with new perspectives and acceptance of inevitable imperfections of life

Acceptance of old career with little interest or enthusiasm; dedication to avocational goals

Continuing distress with no resolution

21

Various attempts can be made to resolve this crisis of alienation. Executives give up lucrative, high-status jobs to do something they always wanted to do. Divorce and the adoption of a new singles life-style, or remarriage, is becoming increasingly common. Sometimes a tolerance for the imperfections of life emerges and the individual is able to rededicate himself to his old career, but with a new, more mature perspective. Another alternative is for the executive to devote himself with fullest enthusiasm to new and exciting avocational pursuits and to simply coast along at the same old job without being engaged by it in any emotional way. Most distressful, and most harmful to both the individual and society, is for no attempted resolution to take place. Then, alienation continues with all the negative fallout it engenders.

LIFE EXPERIENCES

Contradictory life demands

Back in the early 1970s, two sociologists, Richard Sennett and Jonathan Cobb, wrote a book called *The Hidden Injuries of Class*,[17] which had as its major focus an examination of the blue-collar ethnic experience in this country. In particular, they were concerned with how the early years of socialization into a lower working-class ethic affected a person's life-long thoughts and actions. Based principally on extensive interviews with men from this background and their families, the book is full of illustrations of the life-long effects of having been socialized into the working class.

Although most of these interviews are not relevant here, there is a small subgroup of the people interviewed who are of interest because their experiences illustrate the influence of *contradictory life demands*. This group consisted of successful managers from blue-collar Eastern European ethnic backgrounds who were experiencing feelings of personal and social alienation, as were their wives. Why? Their objective condition, financially and status-wise, was far superior to the backgrounds from which they came. Why, then, the personal and social alienation? Sennett and Cobb's research shows that these managers had learned that the attainment of their occupational goals had meant a simultaneous loss of personal affiliative satisfactions.

For these men, the steps leading to this paradoxical outcome began when they were children. Typical of their backgrounds was (1) a family history of low work success in which the fathers were working-class, blue-collar ethnics; (2) a sense of alienation from American society, since they were people of an Eastern European background in a society dominated by a white Anglo-Saxon Protestant culture; and (3) an acceptance of the work-achievement ethic, since this ethic dominated the society to which their families had committed themselves after having left Eastern Europe. As a result of this background, the family instilled a strong desire for upward career mobility in their offspring with the hope that the children could overcome this sense of social alienation from American society and fit into their adopted country.

The promise of career success did not include the contradictory demands of life. There was a failure to see that, for these men, the commitment to work hard in order to be successful and to be accepted meant, at the same time, a denial of family life. One does not, and cannot, have time for everything. This denial of family life generated feelings of aloneness on the part of these upwardly mobile men, who then demanded compensation for these feelings in terms of gratitude from their wives and children. Hadn't they given up their affiliative, family-oriented selves for them? These demands, however, had had an opposite effect from the one intended, in that their requests for gratitude stimulated resentment in their children, who left home at the earliest opportunity. This increased the sense of social alienation on the part of the fathers, and added to the personal alienation they felt at having previously given up their desires for affiliative satisfactions. Furthermore, adding to the sense of alienation of these successful blue-collar managers was their feeling of having lost the social supports of their old family ties and the sense of aloneness that this had generated. They no longer lived in the community they had grown up in, rarely saw old friends and neighbors or their extended families, and felt a sense of estrangement when they did because of their own new and different life-style.

Sennett and Cobb pointed to this phenomenon as being common among the successful managers they studied and suggested that this sense of social loss and personal alienation may be compounded by the individual's feeling that the work he is now doing is not real work which demands of him the craftsmanship and skill he had learned to value as a boy as the hallmarks of a significant job. What did he do now but shuffle papers?

Contradictory life demands become salient as an influence on alienation when the manager realizes that he cannot have it all and that the achievement of one particular goal in life means, at the same time, that he cannot and will not achieve another, *although he believes that he has been promised it all.* This contradiction, and the feeling that one has given up certain personal need satisfactions, is further compounded by the realization that he is not the only one in this predicament. The contradictions that plague him also plague others, who are also not doing all the things they want to do. They are as incomplete as he is in their everyday lives. They have lost both a sense of self (personal alienation) and the ability to relate to and make sense of others (social alienation). In Figure 2 we have outlined several of the sources of contradictory life demands.

The Sennett and Cobb research illustrates one of the most significant of contradictory life demands among managers—the conflict between career and family. Today's manager cannot optimize both. Either a balance is developed, at some cost to both, or one or the other is significantly downgraded. We feel that this is true regardless of what we believe or would like to believe and what our cultural influences tell us. In fact, it is our culture that is one of the major sources of contradiction, according to Chenoweth.[18]

Based on his analyses of the American media and other cultural products, Chenoweth concludes that we can't have it all,

FIGURE 2
Sources of Contradictory Life Demands

Societal factors

Contradictions between:

1. Cultural goals of career success *and* sensory pleasures, religious values, and humanistic values
2. Traditional values of hard work and the postponement of gratification *and* contemporary values of "the future is now" and immediate gratification

Organizational factors

Contradictions between:

1. Hierarchical demands for common unity of work purpose *and* hierarchy-induced subgroup identification and specialization of goals
2. Organizational demands for work commitment *and* family demands for affiliative relationships

→ Contradictory life demands → Realization of inability to satisfy personal need patterns and understand needs of others → Personal and social alienation

25

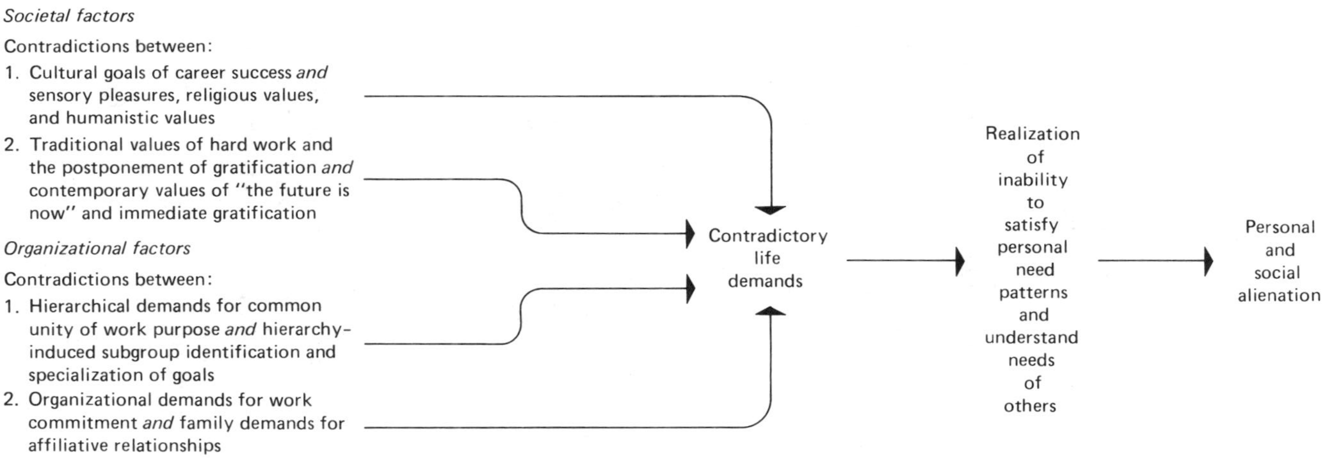

although we are socialized to believe that we can. He proposes that there are four major values (or ethics) in American life that define the goals that we can and should attain. The first of these is the success ethic, which is the feeling that career success and occupational achievement is good and that the more you attain career success, the better. We value good grades in school because this will lead to a good college, and a good college will probably lead to a successful career, and a successful career is desirable because it will lead to a more satisfying life. We therefore move to where the good job is, and we work the hours we need to work to be successful.

The second value we assimilate is our right to happiness. We should try to be happy in a hedonistic sense. Although not everybody in our society agrees that this is a desirable value, it clearly is a goal of great importance for many people. If we look at our media, we see that this goal is probably becoming increasingly important, as is evidenced from most of the social attitude surveys taken in recent years. Its significance is also supported by the fact that the promise of happiness (i.e., money and the pleasure it can bring) is used by most work organizations as a major incentive for encouraging a work/career orientation.

Despite the seeming consistency between these ethics of achievement and hedonism, however, there is good reason to think that this is where the contradictory demands begin in our society. There are social analysts who argue that as our productivity levels reach previously undreamed-of heights and as our corporations encourage the development of those new life ethics which support immediate spending and consumption (so that they may sell their products more profitably), a basic conflict is stimulated in the individual who is career-successful and has achieved at least a moderate level of discretionary income. On the one hand, he works in an organization that has traditionally emphasized rationality, careful planning, and the promise of future happiness; on the other, he is being told (often by the same company) that the future is now, take your happiness now, spend for joy now, and so on. Eventually, he may come to realize that he might have to give up one of these values and that he cannot have them both. Some part of his self will have to be given up, along with his capability for relating effectively to those who have made a decision different from the one he has made.

Among the writers who have focused on this contradiction and its possible implications are Daniel Bell, a sociologist, and George Albee, a psychologist. Each, reflecting his training, has focused on a different aspect of the problem, but their overall thrust is similar. Bell[19] has proposed that the materialistic success of the rational, future-oriented, cognition-stressing economic philosophy that classified men as objects to be organized and integrated with technology and finance into overall systems has, at the same time, generated the free time and energy to stimulate the growth of an anti-rational, anti-intellectual, self-oriented "every man for himself" philosophy that emphasizes immediate sensations of a varied nature. This had led to a personal alienation from our rational, intellectual selves and a sense of social alienation from our rational, intellectual past. The result of all this, Bell writes, is a kind of disjointed social schizophrenia. We live in a double-bind of contradictory messages, not knowing what to do and knowing that regardless of what we choose, we will lose some part of ourselves and/or our cultural linkages. This conflict is also seen by Albee on an individual level.[20] It is his contention that among the reasons for the escalation in the number of people entering therapy is the breakdown of the capitalist-Protestant ethic, which encouraged the repression of sexuality and the delay of personal satisfactions. Our current explosion in productivity has generated more "future is now" thinking and greatly increased spending for personalistic and, often, hedonistic desires. This contradicts our traditional values for hard work and responsibility. It has led, Albee feels, to a loss in our personal and social integration and, as a result, to a dramatic increase in the number of people seeking therapy.

Bell and Albee's proposals are challenging and have some usefulness, but they are somewhat extreme and incomplete. There are other values that can become lost in organizational life besides those reflecting a cognitive, rational way of thinking on one side and egotistic self-indulgence on the other, and these other values might be desirable for individuals, organizations, and society. Cuddihy[21] has suggested that there are certain desirable forms of human emotion that are discordant with the traditional goals of our work organizations in Western society, and that individuals opting to achieve in these organizations have traditionally had to give up the opportunity to express these emotions. Among these emotions, which are far more positive than the egotistical self-indulgence that seems to be implied by Bell and Albee, are (1) the opportunity to express any emotion at all, (2) the acceptance of feelings, (3) an interest in the self and an acceptance of self-examining attitudes as desirable, (4) an acceptance of intimate exposure, and (5) a desire for strong love emotions. In other words, according to Cuddihy, the individual in the organization has needed to give up any desire he might have had to confide in others and any wish to be honest and authentic with others about his feelings. He has had to be, instead, inconspicuous and unemotional. We suggest that when emotions of this nature are surrendered, the sense of personal and social alienation is increased even more.

The desire for career success and the desire for a hedonistic type of gratification are not the only sources of contradictory demands in American society, according to Chenoweth. The manager also learns that he will not be able to satisfy two other major values of American life—religious and humanistic ethics—in any mutually consistent manner. These values are also strong in our culture, and giving them up means losing more of our significant mechanisms for relating to the social world around us.

The religious ethic inspires future-oriented behavior overlaid with humility and caring for others, an emphasis that is antithetical to the "future is now" concept of hedonistic consumption that we are now increasingly encouraging. It is difficult to live a religious life and to simultaneously enjoy the fruits of success in a materialistic way. Of course, one can always change his religion or give it up altogether, as so many upwardly mobile people do. But this serves only to increase the individual's sense of personal and social alienation as he removes himself one step further from a previous source of familial and societal nurturance.

Adding to this sense of contradiction is the fact that managers often feel and accept the necessity and desirability of encouraging immediate spending and consumption in others, if not in themselves, if their companies are to stay in business. Thus, even if the executive remains more modest in his personal spending and consumption habits, he often feels the need to encourage contradictory behavior in others so that his company can remain profitable. This engenders a social alienation from others as a result of his manipulation of them as spending, consuming objects, although the manager in this case remains essentially in touch with his own value system.

Society's humanistic ethic, as discussed by Chenoweth, is also difficult to reconcile with other values, although this, too, is very much a part of our culture. The reasons are not hard to fathom. There seems to be little possibility of reconciling the kinds of behavior that are needed for succeeding in a competitive, hierarchical society such as ours with a humanistic perspective toward others. All our lives we compete with others to get into the best schools, to win games, and to get promotions, knowing all the while that if we get the job, somebody else won't. We are at one and the same time a very career oriented society and a humanistic society. We spend generously on charity, both within our nation and elsewhere in the world, and we maintain strong volunteer institutions. It is difficult for a single individual or group of individuals to do both at the same time. Either one does them at different times in one's life, or one simply drops one of the values. It is hard to adopt a career-success ethic if one wants to be a humanist. The two do not go together.

Being a successful manager does not reduce these conflicts. On the contrary, it may increase the stress, since the manager has originally accepted our social value for career success and met it. However, the norm did not tell him that he would be confronted with these contradictions and he now learns that they come along with his new, more exalted position in life.

There are other sources of disillusionment stemming from contradictory demands for the executive and manager, as Figure 2 points out. We described earlier the emotions of the individuals studied by Sennett and Cobb.[17] They had succeeded in their occupational careers and then found themselves, as part of their new lives, separated from the parents, family, and friends they knew as children. Although the research of Sennett and Cobb is focused mostly on individuals from Eastern European backgrounds whose feelings of loss are magnified by their ethnic heritage and its differences from the primarily Anglo-Saxon culture, these feelings are not limited to such groups. Feelings that career and family needs are hard to satisfy simultaneously are more widespread than this. Seidenberg has shown this to be an increasingly significant source of contradictory life demands for managers in our culture, with one of the most important factors involved being that of geographic mobility.

> There is much to be said for being on the move—it prevents stagnation, promotes adventure, and offers prospects for new opportunities. For many political, religious, and economic refugees, it has meant a new life. For the male in corporate America, it has most often meant challenge and advancement. The man who will not move becomes the deadwood of the company, no longer worthy of serious consideration for top executive positions.
>
> In the moves for enhancement, wives and children usually assent dutifully. Yet such changes of community can have deleterious effects on "helpmates"—the wives who come along for the benefit of their husbands and their families. The hardship for the woman (besides the physical tasks of the move, generally left to the weaker sex) is found in losses that accrue to her in particular, losses not only of friends or neighbors with whom she has grown comfortable but also of status that has come from accomplishment in the community where she resides—the name that she has made for herself in the social and societal sphere if not in a professional role.
>
> In contrast to her husband, whose credentials are easily transferable, her identity as a person, apart from being a wife or a mother, is rarely transferable. In a new community she finds that she must create one all over again. It

is starting from the bottom once more for the most mobile wives—for some again and again. Often they become defeated people, casualties of "success." They are seen clinically during their third and fourth decades of life chronically depressed, lacking in hope or desire, frequently addicted to alcohol, tranquilizers, and barbiturates.

Source: R. Seidenberg, *Corporate Wives—Corporate Casualties?* (Garden City, N.Y.: Anchor Books, Anchor Press/Doubleday & Company, Inc., 1975), Prologue, pp. 1–2 (originally published by AMACOM, New York, 1973.)

This passage illustrates the double-bind that can be generated for an executive by the conflict caused by the kind of mobility he may need for career success and the needs of his family, who can be hurt by it. The opportunity for growth/promotion involved in the move is important. But, for some managers, the happiness of his family is important also, and the problems of a move for his family would be significant. This manager, caught in the squeeze of contradictory life demands, could very easily slip into a major crisis as he realizes that he will have to give up some subset of personal desires that are important to him.

The sense of alienation at the prospect of mobility would be much less for the manager who is either (1) less interested in the promotion, or (2) less concerned with his family's needs, or (3) a member of a family for whom the move is looked upon positively. Such lack of conflict, however, would not necessarily make him less susceptible to other types of contradictory life demands.

We note that although this particular demand of the search for career success among managers and its contradictory aspects have become apparent in recent years and have been subject to considerable discussion by human resource professionals in organizations, much of our cultural media continues to view willingness to relocate and success as being intertwined. In fact, there has been very little questioning of the possibly negative influences of career commitment on family life in general. Even in our newfound openness about divorce, popular culture does not often link the occurrence of a marital split to the demands of a *successful* career.

There are also contradictory demands on the individual manager stemming from his work experience, as well as those coming from the society around him. One of the most important of these is that in the typical work organization he is, at one and the same time, expected to work with other managers and also to compete with them for a share of the always limited available resources. He is pulled toward cooperation with others by the demands of his supervisors and the overall need for organizational success. At the same time, he needs to make himself look good if he is to be evaluated favorably and if his subordinates are to feel secure in their jobs. These demands make him receptive to the need to compete with other managers for his (and his unit's place in the sun. The roles, therefore, are contradictory; one cannot be a cooperator and a competitor at the same time. Yet, this is what the manager is asked to do everyday.

From a variety of perspectives, there are many contradictory life demands on the manager. There is much that he cannot do and much that he cannot attain, even when he very much wants to do so. Being in a managerial role has not guaranteed him immunity from the feelings of personal and social alienation that result from being assailed by contradictory life demands.

Disconfirmed expectancies

> There are two tragedies in life. One is not to get your heart's desire. The other is to get it. Even though a bon mot typical of George Bernard Shaw, perhaps this is a truth that applies to all. No matter how close a person comes to achieving his dream, it will not fulfill all his wishes. The loss of magic that he feels—that everyone feels to some degree in midlife—is the loss of magical hopes attached to the dream when it originally took shape.
>
> (page 278)

The gratification fantasy, boiled down from my discussions

with wunderkinder, goes like this: Once I become president, or full professor, or create the building, the book, the automobile, the film that captures the imagination of our times, people will recognize me, admire me, defer to me. I will be raised aloft like the hero of Saturday's game and allowed to indulge all the desires I have denied myself.

The liberation fantasy would go rather like this: Once I become powerful or rich, no one can criticize or order me around anymore or try to make me feel guilty. I won't have to stand ever again for being treated like a little boy.

The gratification they are really seeking is derivative of the childhood desire to center the world on ourselves and to have all our demands appeased. The liberation they are looking for is freedom from the influence, censorship, and guilt-provoking love of the inner custodian. Above all, there is the vague promise that by becoming masters of their own destiny they will beat even the grim reaper.

What a brutal letdown to discover that this is not so. Success, no matter how grand, does not bring omnipotence. There is always someone who can make us jump. The chairman of the board, the stockholders, the constituency, the advertisers, or someone closer to home, perhaps the aloof adolescent daughter who rules the powerful man with her disdain: "You're an elitist patsy of a corrupt system."

Not only that, colleagues are seldom altogether charitable about a man's success. As Karen Horney noted, "Even the winners in American life feel insecure because they are aware of the mixed admiration and hostility directed at them." Even if the winner's colleagues are not better qualified, many will believe they are, but due to luck or his manipulation of connections or his unsavory tactics or the aesthetic crimes he is willing to commit in the name of commercial success or whatever, he is on top instead of them. They wait for any chance to expose the winner's weaknesses. Many a man who has come a long road to success is deeply saddened by the critical attacks from those very colleagues he expected would recognize and respect him at last.

Nor is it automatic that once a person becomes acclaimed or powerful, the voice of the inner tyrant will be stilled. The work of individuation is internal. We all have to do it unless we prefer to remain very old children. Even when we do finally claim the authority formerly wielded by that inner custodian, we are not only freed but also bereft. We have lost the inner companion who for so many years also made us feel watched over and safe.

(page 279)

Source: G. Sheehy, *Passages: Predictable Crisis of Adult Life* (New York: E. P. Dutton & Co., Inc., 1976).

An expectancy disconfirmation is a problem because it means that one has been out of touch, that he has been wrong in his orientation toward the world. It means that events and plans and decisions do not have the meaning he supposed they had, that people and groups have not acted in the way that he expected, and that the events that he thought were going to take place did not occur. It is a sense of meaninglessness in that he has lost his ability to plan and categorize others and himself. Who are these other people really, if their acts do not match his expectancies? What do their statements mean? What do his own statements mean? What values do his decisions have if they do not lead to what he expected?

An expectancy disconfirmation frequently means that he has not been able to implement an expected aspect of his desires and that an event that he wanted to be part of his life is not going to happen, although he thought and expected and wanted it to happen. The sense of alienation is great, then, whether the expectancy that was disconfirmed had to do with his career desires (personal alienation) or his relationships with others (social alienation).

Underlying the significance of disconfirmed expectancies is the sense of losing one's moorings. Decisions have random implications. All, or parts, of life seem meaningless.

Will alienation occur equally in all managers as a result of a disconfirmed expectancy? Probably not, but it is difficult to pick out why some will feel it worse than others. For most of us, our perspectives of the world and how we structure it are very important. After all, it is such structuring that enables us to predict what will happen and to reduce our anxiety about the possibility of untoward events occurring. This value is the same, independent of the personal enhancement we obtain from the way we have structured the world. The low-self-esteem person, for example, makes choices consistent with his personality structure in order to reduce the anxiety associated with unpredictability, even though an inconsistent choice might result in materially better outcomes.

There is only one possible distinguishing factor that could be identified with reasonable confidence as picking out those individuals for whom the disconfirmation of expectancies might be a greater problem than others. This is the age variable and, in particular, the midlife crisis years. These years are vulnerable ones because of the sense of time passing and declining opportunities. Disconfirmed expectancies are much more significant when there is no infinite future with limitless opportunities ahead.

Disconfirmed expectancies are, therefore, an important source of alienation when they occur. We want to know why they are occurring with increasing frequency among managers. The following summary of *Work, Careers and Social Change* by Seymour Sarason[22] throws some light on this problem.

> At the close of World War II the United States moved into a period of great expectations for the future of our society. While in some respects this growth of optimism and of belief in the future was only an exaggeration of traditional American optimism, the extent of and commitment to this perspective of a positive future reached previously unheard of levels. American optimism also contrasted significantly with the psychological climate of Europe, which had suffered far more in World War II and which realized, as a result, the weaknesses and frailties of many of society's institutions.

Illustrative of these cultural differences were the playwrights popular at the time. In the United States, Arthur Miller's *Death of a Salesman* was the major American work. Its twin themes illustrated a wrong way of life (Willy Loman's), and a *right way*, i.e. the behavioral pattern of the neighbor's son who goes on to an outstanding legal career. The dominant theatre in Europe at the same time was the Theatre of the Absurd, a way of looking at life that recognized and emphasized man's folly, his contradictions, his hypocrisies, and the absurd, mutually contradictory nature of his social institutions. Playwrights such as Beckett, Ionesco and philosophers like Camus were explaining the absurdity of our organizations and our legalities and the folly of trying to make sense of them at the same time that Arthur Miller was stressing that there was a meaning to life and a correct way to proceed. Our task in this country was to find out what that right way was and to follow it.

The expectation that there were correct choices to be made and that life would be satisfying and meaningful if these decisions were made led directly to the legitimatization of the idea that there were certain ways of thinking that were more appropriate, certain schools that had greater value, and certain careers that were more desirable. There was a general growth in the belief that these mechanisms were the path to success and a satisfying life. It is within this context that life was seen as organized and rational and that the concept that there was a way to do things that was right developed. The desirability of certain careers such as medicine, dentistry, corporation executive, etc., became manifest. Schools such as Harvard, Yale, Stanford, etc., became increasingly prestigious. And a great psychological and financial commitment was made to attend these right schools and become part of the high-status, high-success social class. The expectation was that this would guarantee, or at least lead to, a satisfactory and meaningful life.

Unfortunately, there were unexpected results along with the attained successes. Among these was a growth of unrealistic job expectations among successful people stemming from the financial, educational and psychological difficulties inherent in attending these appropriate schools and training for these choice occupations. No school and/or occupation could fulfill the expectations that developed. Secondly, these expectations of (almost) perfection in life if only one made the right choices led to an innocence about the characteristics of the various occupations. No job can provide a consistent diet of rewards. All jobs become routine in some aspects after a while. On the job satisfactions are not always at a high intensity level. All jobs also have negative aspects. Consider the emotions of the doctor who has to deal with death or, less dramatic but still significant, the executive who has to discharge a subordinate.

In addition, these negative feelings become even stronger if the person feels unable to make a change, as is often the case with professionals and executives, since both of these groups have generally made a great financial, psychological, and emotional commitment to their careers. The result of these unrealistic expectations is that the life of the professional and/or executive is rarely what he thought it would be. Feelings of disappointment, alienation, and dissatisfaction are common and pervasive. The situation is made even worse by the fact that the successful person believes that he should not be experiencing unhappiness. Since their lives were supposed to be perfect as a result of having made the right choices, they are unwilling to discuss their newly discovered distress and tend to believe that the alienation they feel means that there is something wrong with them, rather than the world around them. In fact, these feelings are now so pervasive that a rough estimate of individuals making career changes at mid-life despite previous commitments and costs is somewhere between 12 and 20 per cent. It is apparent that this is only the tip of the iceberg. We can only guess at how many others would choose to make changes, if only they dared.

Sarason's observations of disconfirmed expectancies and resulting distress among professionals can also be extended to managers, as Figure 3 indicates. This significance is made even more important by the considerable research evidence that disconfirmed expectancies generate job dissatisfaction and low levels of job performance such as increased turnover.[13] Why is this? One reason is that human beings have as one of their basic motivational drives the desire to achieve outcomes which are consistent with what they know and expect of life and which conform to previously held knowledge. Disconfirmed expectancies create confusion and unhappiness and are not wanted. It is much more comfortable when events that we expect to happen actually happen. When they do not, our uncertainty and anxiety increase.

Involved here, also, with the disconfirmed expectancy is the growth of a sense of meaninglessness. The structure of thought and emotion by which we relate to ourselves and others starts to loosen and we begin to doubt the nature of our perceptions. It becomes difficult to interpret our own behavior and that of others and to grasp what is ephemeral and what is real. If our behavior with others becomes unpredictable in the sense that we do not know what it will lead to, a type of panic results in which the individual loses track of himself and his actions and other people and their actions. Unless we can establish and maintain the kind of meaningful linkages that enable people to function within themselves and with others in a relatively predictable manner, we find feelings of unreality developing along with concomitant increases in personal and social alienation.

One of the most significant disconfirmed expectancies for the manager comes when he realizes that he has lived his life by the promise of the materialistic ethic and finds it to have been an illusion in his case. This is what Milner[23] has called the "Touchstone Fallacy." The materialistic ethic is the belief that the achievement of high occupational and consumer status will, in and of itself, result in a high degree of personal self-actualization, life satisfaction, and a psychological wholeness. When this does not occur, a strong sense of personal and social alienation is

FIGURE 3
Sources of Disconfirmations of Expectancies

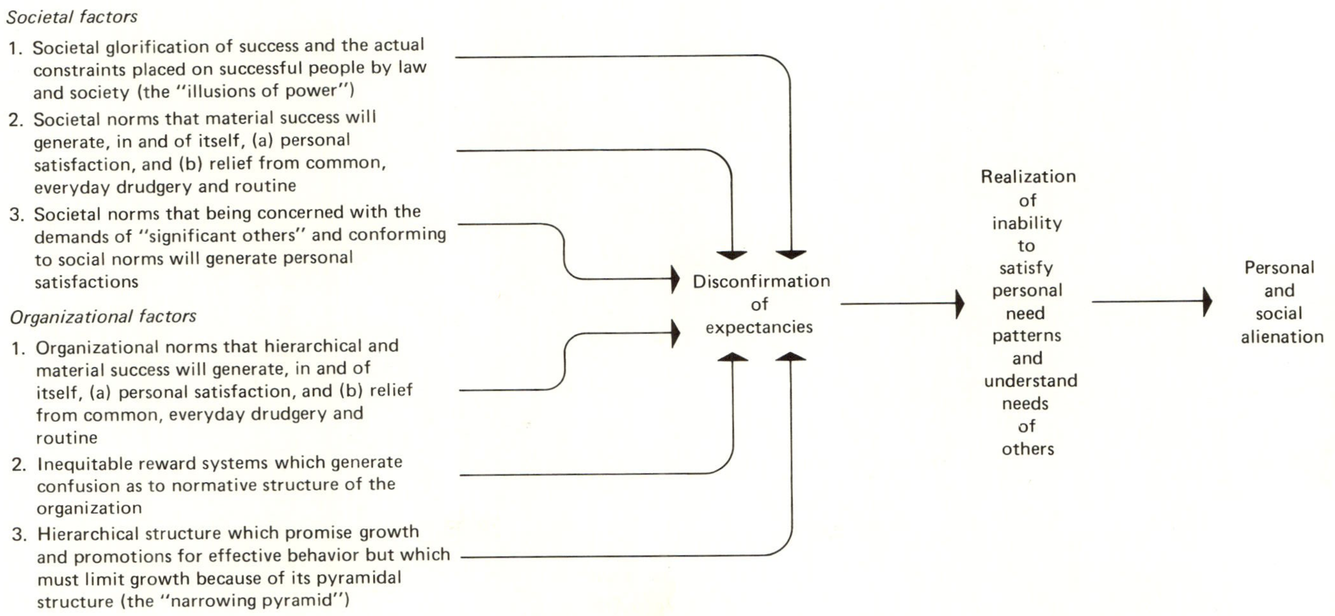

Societal factors

1. Societal glorification of success and the actual constraints placed on successful people by law and society (the "illusions of power")
2. Societal norms that material success will generate, in and of itself, (a) personal satisfaction, and (b) relief from common, everyday drudgery and routine
3. Societal norms that being concerned with the demands of "significant others" and conforming to social norms will generate personal satisfactions

Organizational factors

1. Organizational norms that hierarchical and material success will generate, in and of itself, (a) personal satisfaction, and (b) relief from common, everyday drudgery and routine
2. Inequitable reward systems which generate confusion as to normative structure of the organization
3. Hierarchical structure which promise growth and promotions for effective behavior but which must limit growth because of its pyramidal structure (the "narrowing pyramid")

→ Disconfirmation of expectancies → Realization of inability to satisfy personal need patterns and understand needs of others → Personal and social alienation

39

generated, particularly in the manager, because of the personal investments that are involved in subscribing to the materialistic ethic and because of the importance of this belief to the functioning of our economic and social institutions. After all, more than most occupations, managers have been socialized to believe in and accept the promise of material goods and the desirability of the insititutions that depend on this particular value.

The latter suggests why this particular disconfirmation is often so painful among managers. Milner's analyses of the processes involved here are particularly useful. Her thesis proposes that the adoption of high occupational and consumer status as necessary for psychological wholeness leads us to value and overvalue the gadgets, consumer goods, and status symbols defining such status. Overvaluing these signs of success then generates a loss of a sense of personal control over the course of our individual and collective lives. Since we key ourselves to the symbols, they control us. There is a loss of the belief that human beings are the ultimate arbiters of their lives and the direction of their lives. A sense of competition with others for goods and status is also almost inevitable since the materials valued are limited. In effect, we come to view and judge ourselves and others as essentially acting out a role which has been defined according to the demands of a world that ranks people according to occupational and consumer status and not according to their characteristics as human beings. The result, according to this line of reasoning, is a high degree of personal and social alienation.

We think these predictions as to what happens when we accept the consumer/materialistic ethic can be taken too far and be too extreme in their generalizations. Not all of us accept all of materialism and some of us, even when we accept it for a while, do change and pull back when the negative implications of subscribing to this ethic become too great. Within this limitation, however, a process similar to this does develop among many managers and many do come to think that they have lost their "real selves" and the "real others" in their search for psychological wholeness through material success. (Some illustrations of this are given in Table 1.)

Which managers are most likely to realize their disconfirmed expectancies and their consequent alienated state? They are often men at the midlife stage of their careers. At this time they are most apt to be examining their lives and the guidelines by which they have been living. Who else might be most likely to be feeling this alienation? It is not easy to specify. We would suspect that the thoughtful, introspective individual would be one likely candidate because he might be prone to realize that he did have expectancies at one time in his life and that they have not been realized. Yet, these self-examinations might not necessarily be limited to these individuals, since the realities of life often have a way of presenting themselves and forcing us to pay attention, even to the most unwary. We would conjecture, also, that other factors that might force a self-examination at this time would be the manager's family and friends. The demands and social influences coming from these people would be very likely to have a significant effect on whether an individual manager would go through an introspective examination leading to a possible realization of his disconfirmed expectations and his consequent alienation.

The belief in the personally fulfilling value of increased hierarchical and consumer status is not the only type of disconfirmed expectancy with which a manager has to deal. Another rude shock is often the nature of the managerial role itself, its contemporary characteristics, and, frequently, its unanticipated effects on the emotions and attitudes of the manager himself.

One of the most significant of these unanticipated effects is how the manager sees himself and how he relates to others. David Kipnis, a social psychologist at Temple University, has been responsible for a number of studies that have shown a tendency for powerholders to devalue other people, to maintain distance from others, and, sometimes, to overvalue themselves at the expense of others.

Do managers become managers in order to establish distance from other people and to devalue them? Undoubtedly, some start out with that expectancy in mind, but we seriously question whether this is true of all managers or even most of them. What, then, would be the emotions of a person who finds himself unexpectedly downgrading other people and devaluing them simply because of a position he has attained? Would he start to wonder what kind of person he really was? We think so, particularly if he really doesn't like the idea of devaluing other people for this reason. In addition, his sense of alienation, personal and social, would become even greater as he comes to realize that the tendency he has developed to see people as either high (himself) or low (others) is an incomplete view of both himself and other people. After all, nobody is completely high or low. But how much do you use other factors in judging yourself and others, if being a manager leads you to look at people as either high or low? The answer is not clear. Instead, what we have is an additional unexpected source of alienation as the manager comes to view both himself and others in an incomplete, fragmented manner.

The "burnout" phenomenon[24] is another experience of the managerial job which is usually not expected and which may also operate to increase personal and social alienation.

> Just before Christmas, a woman came to a poverty lawyer to get help. While discussing her problems, she complained about the fact that she was so poor that she was not going to be able to get any Christmas presents for her children. The lawyer, who was a young mother herself, might have been expected to be sympathetic to the woman's plight. Instead, she found herself yelling at the woman, telling her, "So go rob Macy's if you want presents for your kids! And don't come back to see me unless you get caught and need to be defended in court!" Afterwards, in thinking about the incident, the lawyer realized that she had "burned out."
>
> *Source:* C. Maslach, *Burn-Out: The Loss of Human Caring* (Berkeley, Calif.: University of California, Department of Psychology, (1978). (Mimeograph.)

People who have a continuing responsibility for others and who need to treat them with some consideration (as managers do today) eventually begin to feel "burned out" because of the exhaustion that such a responsibility entails. The result is often an alienating detachment from others in self-defense, a greater tendency to pigeonhole them and oneself into categories (since it is easier), and a resulting set of depersonalized relationships, the very essence of personal and social alienation.

Another source of difficulty for the manager today has to do with power, the illusion and the reality. Despite our cultural stereotypes, most managers today only smile at the assumption that they are the bosses of their bailiwick. They are more aware than anyone of the constraints that are being placed on them by governmental agencies at all levels, by labor unions and professional associations, and by massive cultural changes that have led to more independent, authority-resisting attitudes on the part of their subordinates. The so-called joys of being a manager are often not very joyful at all when one is coping with workers who are not very interested or who want a different kind of job or who are unconcerned with promises of rewards and/or punishments, while at the same time keeping aware of governmental regulations which seem to make getting a profitable product on the market next to impossible. Although these facts of the managerial existence do not meet our traditional cultural expectations, they are a fact of life today and bear a major responsibility for the frequent sense of disillusionment found among managers.

"To the victor belongs the spoils" is another cultural adage which we expect to be true in organizations and which the manager often finds disconfirmed with alienating results. Managers are coming to realize that the equity they believed to be a cornerstone principle of organizational life is often illusory. Working hard and doing well may, in fact, not lead to the expected rewards of promotions, salary increases, and power privileges. One reason is the pyramidal shape of the organizational hierarchy. Most managers in a pyramid-shaped organization will inevitably reach a plateau when their upward movement in the system comes to a stop. One can go no further, regardless of the nature of one's performance. Other factors are involved in limiting the correspondence between performance and rewards. They are seniority, strike power, and legal power (affirmative action, etc.). The latter factors, even when they may have nothing to do with competence, may often be the major determinants when the goodies are being awarded. How easy it is, then, for the person who has worked hard and tried his best, to detach himself from his career and the people around him and assume a personally and socially alienated way of looking at the world.

Sense of external control

A classical statement of alienation is sensing that you have not determined the action of your life and the realization that you have been doing things because "they" said to do them or making decisions because *they should be made.* The perception is that the individual has been manipulated and controlled by external forces and that he does not matter. It means that the person one sees behaving everyday isn't oneself at all, which leads to a cognition of personal alienation and a feeling of social alienation from others, since they have not been seeing "the real self." In addition, if there is a belief that others are going through the same processes, behaving in some powerless and unfulfilling way, social alienation increases even further.

One example of external control is being "other-directed," a term coined by David Reisman[25] which describes the feelings of being controlled by the vaguely defined but familiar *they,* as in *they say* or *they do.* Since World War II, many observers of American culture have felt that the term "other-directed" very much fits American society, as opposed to the time prior to the war when individual behavior was controlled much more by an absolute set of standards internalized early in life. People then were "inner-directed" since they used these internalized values as guidelines in making their life choices. However, as massive corporate organizations developed in the postwar period, a higher premium was placed on social skills and understanding others and their desires if one was to work effectively with them. So we became more interested in and more oriented toward understanding and working with others and more responsive to their rules and the requests they might make of us.

Although this change was a new way of thinking, it did not

take long for it to become established, supported as it was by the mass media which stressed, increasingly, that this was the way "to succeed." The result was an acceptance of the principle that one needed to understand the appropriateness of specific activities and values and key oneself to them in planning a life. Such principles were externally defined by the outside world and might vary in different situations, but the important point was that these principles for behavior did exist and that they needed to be paid attention to if one wished to succeed. This was true even if such a sense of being externally controlled generated a sense of powerlessness and even if the external principle was often fluid and changing according to fad, fashion, and demand. (These changes were an additional problem because it was too often the case that one lost sight of what the appropriate principle was in the confused world of changing social norms, with the net result being increased personal and social alienation.)

Another source of the personal and social alienation which results from a sense of powerlessness is experienced in the traditional, pyramid-shaped organizational and social structure. There are several explanations for this.

One view is that of the sociologist Philip Slater. Slater begins by assuming a hierarchical society (i.e., one with different levels and showing a pyramid-type form) and a high value for achievement. These two characteristics, in turn, generate the following outcomes:

1. A desire for individual, rather than group, achievement, because there is decreasing room as one achieves and goes higher in the hierarchical system.
2. A liking for technology and machines, because these can help one achieve.
3. A liking for mastery, power, and control over others, because if one has these, further individual achievement will be more likely.
4. A lack of interest in people as people and an unwillingness to affiliate with other people purely for intrinsic satisfaction, because this will detract from time that

should be directed to achievement and it is harder to compete against friends than against strangers.

Engaging in successful activities reflecting these desires will, according to Slater, generate the development of an attitudinal system supporting such a perspective as the best form of human progress and a rejection of other types of human goals (i.e., those satisfactions derived from meeting family and interpersonal values). There will also be an active disparagement of those who do not subscribe to the technologically oriented model of human progress. To illustrate, this disparagement may take the form of valuing the "lonely hero" who works day and night at his job, rejecting everybody and everything except technological progress. This is a particularly common theme in American literature.

Slater also proposes that the valuation of a technological-growth perspective of human progress generated a personally alienating rejection of certain patterns of need in the self and a socially alienating rejection of the same needs in other people. The needs here being rejected, according to Slater, are:

1. *Communality:* the desire to be with others.
2. *Dependency:* the desire to have others help you in coping with your problems.
3. *Interpersonal competence:* the desire to be effective in coping with interpersonal relations.

Paying attention to one's own non-task-related needs and paying attention to the same needs in others takes time and attention from achieving on an individual basis in a hierarchical society and/or organization. Hence, they are ignored (see Figure 4). This alienation from the self and from others can also lead to such outcomes as:

1. A growth of interpersonal and social problems which are ignored because they detract from individualized achievement and because opportunities exist in our society to run away from interpersonal problems. We run

FIGURE 4

Sources of Sense of External Control

Societal factors

1. Societal norms that being concerned with the demands of "significant others" and conforming to social norms will generate personal satisfactions
2. Unrealistic demands for perfection from the self and others
3. Hierarchical control mechanisms that dictate certain approved behaviors, regardless of personal preferences and desires
4. Media, and interpersonal, examinations of changes in societal guidelines relating to the work ethic, family authority, and religious institutions

Organizational factors

1. Technical demands that control behavior and deny individuality and self-control of behavior choices
2. Incomplete organizational assessments and evaluation practices
3. Demands for control of others and of self, regardless of individuality, which stems from high hierarchical status
4. Hierarchical and bureaucratic demands that (a) routinize behavior and (b) deny individual expression and self-control
5. Unrealistic demands for perfection from the self and others

Sense of external control → Realization of inability to satisfy personal need patterns and understand needs of others → Personal and social alienation

47

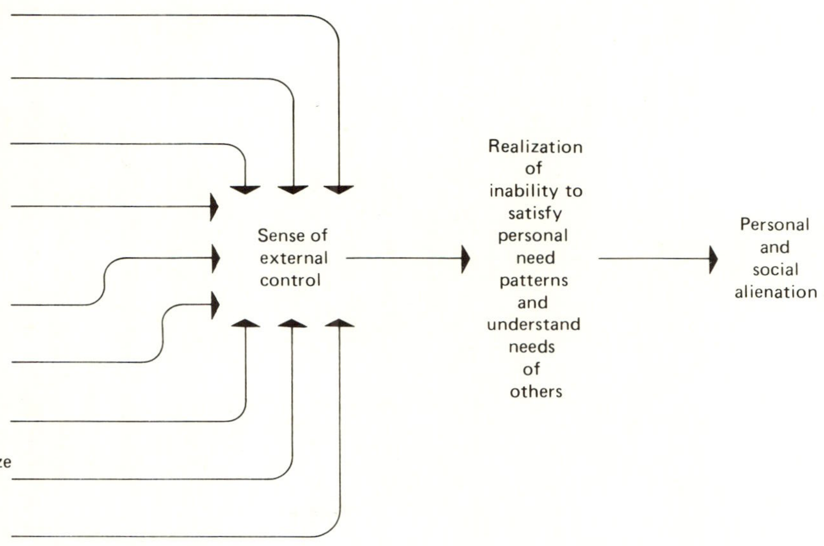

from society's problems by leaving inner cities, and we ridicule personal concerns as not being businesslike.
2. The development of plans for resolving interpersonal problems which are nonfunctional and unlikely to resolve the problems. This only makes the problems worse.
3. An ignorance of interpersonal concerns in general and a rejection of personal and social needs as a basis for decision making. This neglect of personal desires tends to lead to decisions that are (a) not accepted by the people involved, (b) more likely to lead to conflict and less effective coordination, and (c) likely to be even more superficial and generate even more alienation in the future.

There is good evidence for Slater's arguments in many research studies. Loss of a sense of self and a growth of aggression and conflict is often a result of being encapsulated in a pyramid-shaped hierarchical structure. Furthermore, the effects are often cumulative over time; the longer one is part of the structure, the worse it is. In addition, there is also support for Slater's argument in the frequent findings of a lower desire for affiliation and greater interpersonal alienation among men (to whom the derivation above is meant to apply) than among women (for whom different processes are proposed).

Slater is not alone is predicting that pyramid-shaped hierarchies generate a sense of personal and social alienation in individuals who spend time in them. Korman[27] has proposed that people make choices in a manner that is consistent with how they feel about themselves and other people. A person who has high self-esteem chooses social roles that are consistent with this perception. That is, they seek ways to satisfy their needs and meet their personal desires since meeting personal needs is consistent with high self-esteem. The high-self-esteem person, in terms of our concerns here, is not alienated from his needs (i.e., he is sensitive to them and looks for ways to satisfy them). Similarly, the person who has high esteem for others is sensitive to their needs and tries to meet them (i.e., he is not alienated from them). On the other hand, the individual with low self-esteem and low esteem for others makes choices which are both personally and socially alienating. That is, they ignore their own needs when making their choices, and they ignore the needs of others when interacting with them.

Of importance to us here is that self-esteem and esteem for others appear very clearly to be a result of one's type of hierarchical experience. Those who have spent time in organizations or other types of social systems with pyramid-shaped hierarchies learn that both they and others are undesirable, since if they were not, there would be little need to be externally controlled. The result is low self-esteem, low esteem for others, and personal and social alienation. On the other hand, situations of low hierarchical control generate just the opposite feeling (i.e., high self-esteem, esteem for others, and low personal and social alienation).

Regardless of which theory one finds most appealing as a theoretical means of explanation, the significance of continuing exposure to pyramid-shaped hierarchies as a source of personal and social alienation appears to be well established. However, it is by no means the only type of work experience which stimulates feelings of powerlessness in the executive-manager. Another source stems from the fact that at this time the managerial world is a masculine world in a traditional sense. It is full of the prejudices, connotations, and motivations that mark such a perspective and of the social pressures that go along with these norms. One such norm is the demand for perfection or, in its alternative terminology, the fear of failure. We do not know where or why this type of motivational process became so paramount as an external demand influencing the lives of American managers (males), but paramount it is. Perhaps it developed because of the belief in the American dream that there was an opportunity for all to get ahead in American society, although this was always more apparent than real for most people. The fact that the opportunity for vertical mobility has always been most real for white males has, possibly, made failure most frightening to them, since they could not blame their failure on others but had to accept it as a personal fault.* Perhaps, also, failure has always been most frightening to American males because they carried with themselves the projected goals and aspirations of their immigrant forebears who had come to America to seek their fortunes. Having found the streets not paved with gold, they set about making their children into the successes they had dreamed of becoming. For the children, failing would be failing them and, perhaps, becoming rejected by them.

Perhaps, also, the fear of failure might be connected to the great emphasis on sexuality in American life. Since male sexual failure is more apparent than the failure of the female, it is possible that men may fear impotence more and that this might generalize to the work setting. After all, do not many Americans view sexual activity as a form of performance? Note, also, that winning at sports can be considered in a similar vein, and what is emphasized more in sports than not losing (or not failing)?

Whatever the reasons, and there may be more than these, fear of failure is a significant type of social demand which operates as a mechanism for external control on most American males. It is supported even further by the business organization, a social institution which is, after all, also competitive, offers (some) vertical mobility, and is intensely masculine. Its significance for us here is that the fear of failure, as an internalized form of social control and as a norm supported by most business organizations, generates a hiding of oneself so that one denies both to oneself and to others any sign of the (nondesirable) characteristics associated with weakness or failure. Thus, we

---

*We might note that the similarity between the notions of traditional maleness and the managerial world is not changing very much, even with the rapidly increasing number of female managers. Most of the articles being written, books published, and seminars conducted are designed to enable the aspiring female executive to overcome some of the traditional motivational characteristics of women (i.e., the fear of career success and the lack of assertiveness) and to act like traditional men. However, traditional men also have motivational problems (i.e., the fear of failure), and there is little reason to regard them as models to be emulated uncritically.

would predict that a high-fear-of-failure manager would (1) resist any type of concrete, realistic performance appraisal, (2) turn performance demands into bureaucratic chores of little relevance to actual task requirements, (3) surround himself with people who cannot provide him with any realistic appraisal of his own ideas and characteristics, and (4) make decisions which involve either no risk at all or which involve risks virtually doomed to failure because they are beyond the capabilities of anyone so that no one can be blamed for failing at them. These patterns of behavior are obviously greatly dysfunctional for organizational effectiveness, an effect that becomes cumulative over time because the individual who is gripped by the fear of failure rarely makes choices that will enable him to learn anything negative about himself or his choices.

Being in the grip of the fear-of-failure ideology also leads the individual to view himself (and others) as performing machines and things, rather than as human beings with all the strengths and weaknesses that being human implies. The result is even greater personal and social alienation. Do we really believe ourselves to be machines? I doubt that many of us do completely. Yet, to the extent that we adopt this perspective as *the way we should be* and *the way others should be*, we develop an incomplete, unreal perspective on how we and others are and, in that context, we deny our own humanity and the humanity of others.

We are not suggesting here that the desire to do well is bad. It isn't: not for society, not for organizations, and not for individuals. It can be a great source of personal and material satisfaction. However, when it becomes a demand for perfection it generates a requirement that we dissociate ourselves from everything about ourselves and others which is not perfect. We lose a sense of ourselves and a sense of others. They cannot get to know and understand us to the degree we would like and we cannot get to know them.

Perhaps one answer to this apparent conflict is to begin assimilating into our culture some of what Novak[28] has called "Mediterranean cynicism." He proposes that while we should not try to do away with our drives toward individual and economic growth, we should, in the interests of reducing our anxieties and our alienation, leaven our dreams and aspirations with a little reality and a little objectivity. This reality and objectivity includes the need to accept such factors as:

1. Individuals (including yourself) may be weak, corrupt, and selfish as well as good. People try to control as well as to help one another.
2. Institutions are not inherently more or less corrupt than individuals. Both have good and bad aspects.
3. All interpersonal agreements involve payoffs and self-interest as well as common goals.
4. Nothing is all good or all bad. The costs in what appears to be a positive outcome may just be hidden for a while.
5. It is not necessary to always have a winner and a loser. Everybody may win at one level or another in many interpersonal and group disputes.

Novak feels that this dose of reality, which residents of Spain, Italy, and other Mediterranean countries have learned in their long, often-tormented histories, should be combined with the urge to individual achievement and vertical mobility which is so much part of our American heritage. The result would be less of a need for perfection and a greater acceptance and knowledge of ourselves and others. It is a point of view that makes a great deal of sense.

The acceptance of the accumulation of material goods as a measure of individual evaluation contributes also to a sense of powerlessness as well as to the feelings of disconfirmed expectancies we discussed earlier. Consider, for example, the following items for their potential impact on how you might view yourself (and others):

1. The size and location of your office.
2. The amount and type of carpeting on your floor.

3. Your neighborhood.
4. Your house.
5. The car(s) you drive.
6. The schools your children attend.

A major form of external control that many of us feel is that the traditional materialistic norms lead us to want to get the biggest and best ratings on the items listed above if we are to think well of ourselves. The norm is greatly supported by our mass media and educational systems both indirectly and directly. In *Something Happened,* Joseph Heller describes the process of moving from house to house as a veritable compulsion as one climbs the organizational ladder. One car manufacturer advertises a newly styled model as looking like and being mistaken for a higher-priced automobile. This supposedly confers higher status on its owner who is treated better by parking lot attendants and others because they think he is driving the more expensive car.

As a form of external control influencing a loss of a sense of self and a growth of personal and social alienation, this process may be one of the most destructive. Moving to a new house because of the requirements of some vague others, even if one is happy with the old house, is the beginning of depersonalization. There is always a bigger house to aspire to and there are always more expensive cars. A Rolls-Royce is more expensive than a Mercedes, and a custom-built Maserati is even more costly. To be oriented toward such continued striving *when* the old house and Ford were fine all along is the essence of being externally controlled and denying your sense of self.

The student rebels of the 1960s were among the first to begin to define the incongruousness and alienating effects of this life-style, and although they have disappeared for the most part, their impact has remained. Now it has spread to their older brothers and sisters and their parents, contributing to the growth of management alienation by pointing to the possible discrepancies between what an individual feels he wants out of life and the material rewards for which he is supposedly working. The two often are not the same and when the manager sees the fallacy and alienating effects of a continued striving for external rewards that he isn't quite sure he wants, his work begins to lose meaning since all it is doing is providing him with a mechanism for achieving goals that are no longer relevant for him.

The 40-year-old vice-president of a large company in Southern California recently shocked his colleagues by leaving his job, giving up his beautiful home and all the other goodies he had acquired as a result of his success, and purchasing a farm in Texas. What's more, three of his boyhood friends joined him in giving up their careers and purchasing adjoining farms, thus fulfilling a childhood dream that all had long since pushed aside. The (ex)vice-president is now working as a farmer, putting in 14 to 16 hours a day of strong physical labor. His superiors and peers still don't understand what happened, and they talk about it wonderingly. The younger managers, however, may have gotten a different message. Perhaps for some of them the maverick vice-president is more of a model than those who remained and who continue to prefer the golf, tennis, and other privileges and prerogatives that have become so much part of the affluent, successful life-style in contemporary America.

We do not mean to imply that most younger (or older) Americans may be thinking of giving up the life-style that many of us enjoy. Air conditioning in the summer, electric knives to carve our turkeys, and color television sets to amuse us are all part of our lives today. Indeed, families on welfare are frequently supplied with funds to purchase TV sets and to live in buildings with elevators, electric washing machines and dryers, and other types of labor-saving devices. However, the crucial significance of these factors to determine life choices is beginning to lessen for many people. We know that life goes on regardless of whether one drives a Ford or a Mercedes, and the organizations we work for have to increasingly deal with these emerging sets of attitudes.

Most managers are not as alienated as the aforementioned farmer apparently was. At this time, it is probably only a minority who are at the level of first coming to realize how materialistic object accumulation as a controlling influence affects how they make choices, how they view themselves, and how they view others. They are only beginning to wonder if life is just accumulating one more expensive object after another. Some years ago there was a program on national television which recounted the life of a successful bank executive in the Midwest who lived in an affluent suburb. After considerable discussion of his personal doubts and difficulties and an examination of a disturbing sense of alienation among the members of his family (including himself), the program concluded by showing how the family attempted to resolve their difficulties by moving to an even more affluent suburb. This program, and the spectacular television examination of the Loud family of Santa Barbara, California,* were discussed by us with a number of executive groups and we found their reactions to be mutually contradictory and very much reflective of the confusion in many executive lives today. They agreed that:

1. It is very self-destructive to think that the only thing in life is to accumulate possessions, but what else is there?
2. People who spend their lives running after swimming pools and new cars sometimes forget to ask themselves if they really want them and what they'll do with them once they get them and the novelty has worn off.
3. People who are always seeking the new car and the new house tend to think that other people are just like them. The result is that all these people can and do talk about is the acquisition of things. Problems are forgotten, emotions are not dealt with, and there is a gamelike, unreal quality to the way they talk to one another. Yet, this is what life is like according to the managers and, according to them, it is perfectly understandable to be controlled in your life by materialistic goals.

*You will recall that this was an examination of the life-style of an affluent, materialistic family. During the course of the program, the infidelities of the husband became exposed, a divorce was agreed upon, the eldest son declared his homosexuality, and a general emptiness of life was apparent.

The contradictions in the attitudes and perspectives of these managers seem apparent. Living in our materialistic society they have learned that the possession of these goods does serve as a mechanism for evaluating oneself and others, although they may serve as an external control mechanism and a way of alienating us from our sense of self and from others. We do make evaluations on this basis and we do believe, as a society, that those who have more of these things are better off (and better) than those who have less. Yet, the more we make these judgments and evaluations, the more we are unconsciously denegrating the value of individual desires and preferences and the more we are denying the significance of individuals, individuality, and humanity in general.

Technology is, in certain respects, like a consumer good in that we develop technological innovations as mechanisms toward greater achievement (or work satisfaction) in the same way that we cite or propose a consumer good as a mechanism for achieving a more personal satisfaction. The problems, therefore, are quite similar. The growth of technological innovations as mechanisms for achieving certain outcomes leads to a value for the mechanism in and of itself and a consequent personal and social alienation. Technology, once developed, serves to control choice patterns and work strategies as we seek to adapt our lives to the machines that we originally developed as arms to aid us in our adaptation but which now dictate strategies to us in order that we may help them work better. They may dictate whom to hire, how to train them, and the patterns of work behavior that are most appropriate. In brief, the machine (or consumer good) that we started out controlling is now controlling us, with all the consequences for personal and social alienation which this entails.

An illustration of the indictments that have been made against technology as a cause of personal and social alienation is given in the work of Yablonsky,[29] who coined the term *Robopaths* as the title for his book. According to Yablonsky, the robopath is a person who has been socialized in a highly technological environment and who can be described as:

Ritualistic: people who are programmed and preplanned and who deny themselves in the interests of plans and programs.

Oriented to the past: people who are oriented to the past (for which they have developed their plans originally) and who reject the contemporary world (for which they have no plans).

Conformist: people who fear anything new or different because they have no programs for handling them.

Involved with their image: people who make sure that their public presentation matches socially appropriate rules and programs rather than individualistic needs or desires (which may or may not be socially acceptable).

Acompassioniate: people who act toward others according to rules and programs rather than emotions or moral values.

Hostile and morally corrupt: people who will accept hostility and moral corruption as long as they are dictated by the appropriate set of rules.

Self-righteous: people who believe that their behavior is always right, regardless of how it appears, since they always act according to the proper rules and procedures.

Overall, then, the robopath perspective states that technology generates alienation because it is an external control system which emphasizes extensive preprogramming of people and extensive rules instead of relying upon individuality and self-control.

Technology also generates personal and social alienation because it stimulates changes in the social system and, as a consequence, people lose their sense of bearing. All social systems have inherent strains as a result of the inevitable discrepancies between the ideals they set up to justify themselves and the actual realities in which they exist. There is always some alienation as people realize that they are rarely able to completely fulfill the ideals that originally stimulated them to get involved in an activity or to truly understand the needs and desires of the other people in the system. Technological changes generate personal and social alienation by disorienting people as they lose their ability to place themselves and other people when social norms begin to break down as a result of change. The social cues we have used to help us guide our lives lose their meaning and we find it increasingly difficult to judge ourselves and to judge others.

It should also be noted that it has been claimed that technology can exacerbate the values that separate people and cause social alienation by increasing, through financial and work-time commitment, an individual's overvaluation of a particular perspective and an undervaluation of other points of view.

These arguments, although of great value and worth considering, may be too extreme. The dangers of technology generating massive alienation can be exaggerated. People are not that pliable and susceptible to social influence—they can and do revolt, sometimes quite successfully. Granting this, however, the fact remains that technology may well be a significant source of alienation. Surprisingly, this is particularly true among those whom we do not normally think of as being affected by technology in their everyday working lives (i.e., managers and executives). We must realize, however, that managers do use technology as an extension of themselves (e.g., the utilization of computers), and they may be subject to merging their views of themselves with their views of the technology they are using and becoming one with it. To be melodramatic, the machine may become the man and the man may become the machine.

Another source of external control that results in a sense of powerlessness and personal and social alienation is the general feeling that results when one thinks he is at the mercy of forces beyond his control. There are a number of ways in which this can happen. One keeps reading in the newspapers and hearing and seeing on television that the world is changing, institutions are collapsing, guidelines are no longer relevant, and, most important, we can do nothing about these phenomena. They are going to affect each individual life, whether we like it or not. Such a sense of being manipulated has a very good likelihood of creating a feeling of personal and social alienation. How confident can one person feel that he will be able to act according to his desires and needs and also understand the feelings of others when he is at the mercy of mass, unnamed influences and factors beyond his control?

This is the type of feeling that is most likely to occur in those large organizations that do not have meaningful, accurate assessment and performance appraisal systems. It is the reason that we believe that the need is overwhelming to provide individual managers with concrete feedback as to whom and what they are in the company, where they can go, and what they may expect to do. For most of them, when the dissemination of this information is not the practice, there is the impression that they are at the mercy of mass impersonal forces of a noncontrollable nature. It is no wonder that many of these people have little hope of ever doing what they would really like to do and of thinking that they will be able to do what they would choose to do. Instead, the perspective that develops among them is one wherein they play a game designed not to offend the unseen forces and to be acceptable to the greatest number of people. As a result, the person may need to and often does deny his own needs and the needs of others. This is one of the costs we pay for ignoring our need for knowledge of ourselves and our capabilities.

Fortunately, this problem may be decreasing if we can interpret the great interest of companies in performance appraisal programs today as a criterion. Also part of this trend is the utilization of overall assessments of personal capability through the appropriate use of personality measures (objective and projective), group exercises, personal interviews, and simulation tasks. All of these mechanisms, when used correctly, enable us to develop a measurable, realistic picture of individual competencies and capabilities. These descriptions operate for the benefit of both the individual and the organization because they facilitate the reduction of the individual's anxieties concerning the arbitrary nature of the world around him and the alienation he feels as a result of his attempt to meet the unknown demands of these feared authority figures. They also enable the company to do a better job of rational job assignments and placements. Later in this book we will discuss more completely the nature of these assessments and performance appraisal programs.

Loss of Affiliative Satisfactions

The new industrial leader is not as hardhearted as the autocratic empire builder, nor is he as dependent on the company as the organization man. But he is more detached and emotionally inaccessible than either. And he is troubled by that fact: he recognizes that his work develops his head but not his heart.

(page 98)

Careerism demands detachments. To succeed in school, the child needs to detach himself from a crippling fear of failure. To sell himself, he detaches himself from feelings of shame and humiliation. To compete and win, he detaches himself from compassion for the losers. To devote himself to success at work, he detaches himself from family.

As a result, high-ranking corporate managers exercise and develop many positive intellectual characteristics while their emotional qualities tend to atrophy. They lack passion and compassion. They are cool or lukewarm. They are emotionally cautious and protected against intense experience. The process of bending one's will to corporate goals and moving up the hierarchy leads to meanness and stinginess.

(page 104)

Source: M. Maccoby, The corporate climber, *Fortune,* December 1976.

She sounded angry and bitter. As she sat smoking one cigarette after another in an assertiveness training class, the 37-year-old suburban housewife spat out the words, "I'm never going to move again. There's no reason for me to do it any more. I've been married 18 years, and for a long time we were transferred every two years, and I'm finished. The price is too high."

Then, glancing away, she added, "I even had a love affair—which ended very unhappily—when we were living in New York three years ago. I know it happened because of all those uprootings and because my husband had become such a corporation man and traveled so much he rarely spent any time with our children and me.

I also resented the fact that I was never consulted about those moves. The company gave the order, my husband came home and told me about it, and I had to pack, make all the arrangements and follow him."

She seemed to calm down, her voice dropping lower, as she continued, "They always gave him a promotion, with a new title, a bigger salary and more responsibility. They paid all our moving expenses. But the toll on our marriage and on our adolescent and teen-age kids was tremendous.

My husband always went to his new office and got involved immediately. But I couldn't transfer my credentials, and our children couldn't either. We had to start all over each time, trying to make new friends, finding an identity for ourselves.

And when I finally began to realize how I felt, and insisted we talk about it, we began to look at moving as a family, now that we've finally assessed the pros and cons, and talked about how we all really felt, we'll never do it again."

This delicate blond suburbanite, dressed in her wrap skirt, neat blouse and canvas espadrilles, is not alone. Ticor Relocation Management Co. recently made a survey of 617 companies and found that only 4 per cent of their employees refused job transfers in 1974. The figure jumped to 42 per cent in 1975.

More and more corporation nomads are taking a closer look at the quality of their lives and refusing to budge. They're asking if it's really necessary to move in order to move up.

Source: Why corporate nomads are rebelling, *San Francisco Examiner,* August 24, 1977, p. 61.

The loss of affiliative satisfactions is fast becoming recognized as one of the greatest sources of personal and social alienation among managers. Paradoxically, this is also a type of loss that many of our traditional cultural norms have prescribed as being insignificant and unimportant for males. It is, in fact, not seen as very important by many men in their 20s and 30s, although this may be changing slightly today. However, there is little question that these needs do become more salient as the individual ages. One of the most commonly reported sources of distress for the manager in his 40s and 50s is his alienation from his family and the overall lack of meaningful interpersonal relations in his life. The *ability to relate* and the *need to relate* seem to be the war cries of our times and at the very center of those chanting the slogans is, increasingly, the middle-aged manager.

What generates this sense of loss and alienation? First, there are the inevitable developmental changes in people, factors we will review in the next chapter. Then, as we indicate in Figure 5, there is the mobility problem, a factor that increases personal and social alienation in a variety of ways, as we discussed earlier. It is only recently that we have begun to see how much of a problem this can be. Perhaps the tardiness in recognition is understandable, considering the intimate connections that we have always seen among career success, personal happiness, and our great cultural emphasis on achievement. *I'll go wherever the job is* was a slogan for two decades of ambitious young Americans. And they did! With their wives and children following dutifully behind them because they, too, believed in that value. Or, at least, the wife did. The children usually weren't asked. From the viewpoint of personal and societal work success, the advice was, and probably still is, good. However, there has been a cost. We are only now beginning to recognize how great a cost it has been. Mobility has generated among many a sense of loss in psychological and social mooring and, increasingly, a reference to the ties that have been lost and a desire for their reestablishment. The operations manager of a food manufacturing plant told us that the most satisfying aspects of his life at this time were the Polish-

FIGURE 5
Sources of Loss of Affiliative Satisfaction

Societal factors
1. Geographic mobility and dispersion of families
2. Media, and interpersonal, examinations of changes in societal norms relating to family life and traditional social institutions (e.g., religious institutions)

Organizational factors
1. Geographic mobility and dispersion of families
2. Organizational conflict resulting from subgroup identification with resulting goal specialization and the need to compete for scarce resources
3. Hierarchical and bureaucratic demands that limit opportunities for interaction to rational, task-oriented activities

→ Loss of affiliative satisfaction → Realization of inability to satisfy certain personal need patterns and understand the needs of others → Personal and social alienation

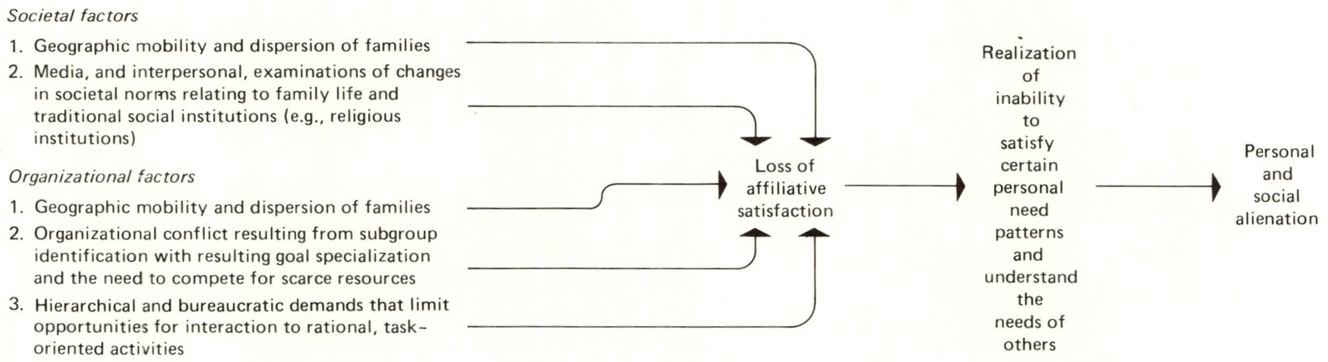

American festivals he and his family attended several times a year. This manager is in his mid-40s and indicated little reluctance in discussing the emotional value that this tie to his ethnic heritage had for him. It is not surprising that one of the most rapidly growing problems among multilocation corporations is the reluctance of some managers to make geographic moves, even when the move involves a pay increase and/or promotion.

We should keep in mind, however, that this reluctance is a relatively new phenomenon and that for many managers the loss of affiliative satisfactions has already occurred. They have gone through the challenges and the problems of the geographic moves, and it is the problems with which they now need to deal. There are the broken marriages, the alcoholic wives, the children who are strangers, the lack of friends on whom they can count in a pinch, the few people with whom they can share their joys and their sorrows, and the paucity of people who see and know and appreciate them for what they are as human beings rather than for the material and occupational levels they present toward the world. All of these contribute to a loss of a social network within which to place oneself and within which to obtain affiliative satisfactions and social nourishment. Personal and social alienation are almost inevitable in such a situation.

A second factor generating a loss of affiliative satisfaction is the pyramid type organization structure and the competition it promotes for personal advancement, for resources, and for visibility. One problem of a pyramid-shaped hierarchy is that, by definition, there is less room available the higher one goes in the system and this generates a competitiveness, and often conflict, among those who are fighting for the rewards. The implication of this conflict is that we may come to see other people in the organization not as real, complex people but as enemies, current and potential, against whom one must compete. Similarly, one comes to look upon oneself as a competitor, not a complex individual with a variety of needs, feelings, and interests. Obviously, this is hardly a situation that discourages alienation.

Working in a bureaucratic system with its routinization and procedural directions is also a contributing factor in the loss of affiliative satisfactions. Yablonsky's work on robopaths, discussed earlier, is illustrative of this process.

Finally, there is the feeling of losing touch with others and the self that arises from the mass media's continuing focus on the decline of those social institutions that tied together the lives of most Americans two decades ago. The decline of religious institutions, the loss of faith in government and the professions, and the continuing disintegration of American family life have all become favorite topics for exploration in the worlds of television, newspapers, and magazines. The cumulative impact of these reports may be to make the individuals reading and seeing them feel they have lost some of those social relationships that used to bind them to other groups and people and which enabled them to place themselves more accurately and meaningfully in the social context. Now, as they keep reading that their social cues are disappearing, their own sense of personal and social alienation keeps increasing.

THE MALE MID-LIFE STAGE AS AN INFLUENCE ON MANAGEMENT ALIENATION

What then is the psychological nature of this reaction to the mid-life situation, and how is it to be explained?

The simple fact of the situation is the arrival at the mid-point of life. What is simple from the point of view of chronology, however, is not so simple psychologically. The individual has stopped growing up, and has begun to grow old. A new set of external circumstances has to be met. The first phase of adult life has been lived. Family and occupation have become established (or ought to have become established unless the individual's adjustment has gone seriously awry); parents have grown old, and children are on the threshold of adulthood. Youth and childhood are past and gone, and demand to be mourned. The achievement of mature and independent adulthood presents itself as the main psychological task. The paradox is that of entering the prime of life, the stage of fulfillment, but at the same time the prime and fulfillment are dated. Death lies beyond.

I believe, and shall try to demonstrate, that it is this fact of the entry upon the psychological scene of the reality and inevitability of one's own eventual personal death that is the central and crucial feature of the mid-life phase—the feature which precipitates the critical nature of the period.

Source: E. Jacques, *Work, Creativity and Social Justice* (New York: International Universities Press, 1970), pp. 47–48.

Are you:

Aware of your advancing age?

Aware of the aging of your friends? your parents?

Aware of all of the satisfactions and goals you will never attain?

Becoming aware of new goals?

Becoming aware of some of your old goals and how, after years of not thinking about them, they have suddenly become important to you?

Aware of changes in your wife? your children?

Afraid that you are becoming obsolescent in your position?

Afraid that you have decreased opportunities for promotions and greater future job rewards?

If your answer to all or most of these questions is yes, you are in a phase of your life that has come to be known as midlife. This phase is very important to us here because there is reason to think that even if a particular manager is exposed to only a minimal number of the factors we have discussed in the previous pages, he is still likely to feel some sense of personal and social alienation by the time he reaches his mid-40s. Until recently, society assumed (or hoped) that the adult years were a stable plateau, an assumption that was needed to justify the fact that our most important social institutions traditionally have demanded lifetime (marital and vocational) choices in the early 20s. After all, if the adult years were not stable, then the making of lifetime choices in the early 20s was difficult to defend, as was the difficulty of defending educational and vocational institutions which make it so hard to change careers at midlife. We have now come to see the adult years as far less stable than we thought, as a time of dynamic changes in many instances, and as a process that generates certain regular patterns of decision making as the person ages. Most specifically, for our purposes, we now know that a particularly significant time is the decade beginning around age 40, or the midlife phase.

In Figure 6 we have outlined a distillation of recent research on the adult life stages and some of the particular problems of the male at midlife. The chart illustrates why this particular development stage is so important for understanding personal and social alienation among managers. It is at this time that:

1. One perceives that life has become a narrowing process. This can lead to conflict with others for whom life choices have not as yet narrowed.
2. One is most likely to believe that his actual career has not matched his career ideal (as it almost never does), thereby generating a sense of personal loss and personal alienation.
3. One realizes that mobility as a mechanism for eliminating frustration is decreasing, as is the possibility that there will be future rewards as compensation for the problems of the past. This can also generate a strong sense of personal and social alienation.
4. One becomes aware of a decline in physical energy, efficiency, and physical appearance, compared to what one once was. This can create a debilitating sense of personal loss and alienation.

All of these may operate to remind the individual manager

FIGURE 6
Developmental Sources of Career Success and Personal Failure

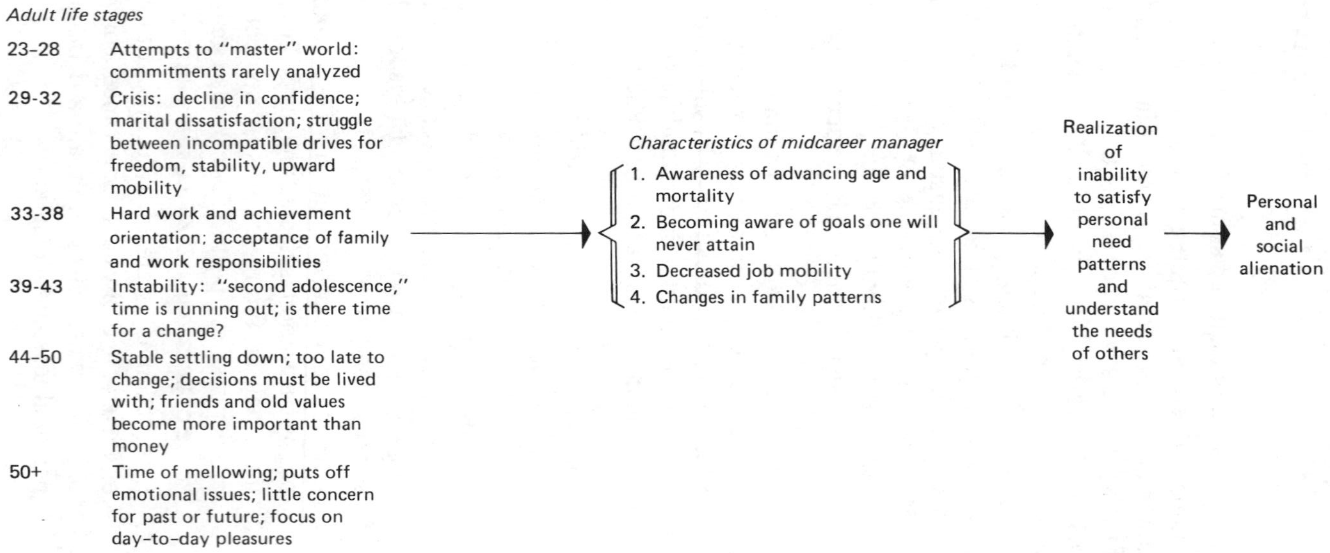

Adult life stages

23-28	Attempts to "master" world: commitments rarely analyzed
29-32	Crisis: decline in confidence; marital dissatisfaction; struggle between incompatible drives for freedom, stability, upward mobility
33-38	Hard work and achievement orientation; acceptance of family and work responsibilities
39-43	Instability; "second adolescence," time is running out; is there time for a change?
44-50	Stable settling down; too late to change; decisions must be lived with; friends and old values become more important than money
50+	Time of mellowing; puts off emotional issues; little concern for past or future; focus on day-to-day pleasures

Characteristics of midcareer manager

1. Awareness of advancing age and mortality
2. Becoming aware of goals one will never attain
3. Decreased job mobility
4. Changes in family patterns

↓

Realization of inability to satisfy personal need patterns and understand the needs of others

↓

Personal and social alienation

that he is at a time in life when the discrepancy between his reality and his dreams has become too concrete to ignore and that the amount of time for reconciliation of the two is limited, if it is to take place at all. It is no wonder, then, that a sense of personal alienation becomes so common at this point in life, as does a sense that if one has only been playing a game until now, so has everyone else (probably). Thus, it is not only the self that is remote; it is other people also. They have not been acting any more real than the self.

Of significant importance to the organization is that the emotions which are generated at this time have considerable impact on the achievement motivation of the individual manager. Often, the changes that emerge in the manager as he seeks to deal with these new views of himself and others is to move away from his traditional work orientation and toward other means of satisfaction. The fact is that by age 40 much of life has happened in the past. Marriage has taken place, children have been born, career choices have been made. We can no longer look forward to these events—they are in the past. We become increasingly conscious of our own mortality as gray hairs and middle-age spread become apparent. Elderly parents have become ill or died. It is at about this time that the life process, which has been going on all along, hits the individual with a wallop and a great sense of personal and social alienation is often the result.

Gould's[30] research is useful in illustrating this entire perspective. Utilizing data gathered from 524 white middle-class people, he found that:

1. As people pass the age of 40, they increasingly feel that it is too late to make major career changes. They try to be satisfied with what they have and think less about what they don't have. Their major concern becomes health. They realize that they would feel lost without their friends. Their children become more important to them than ever.
2. As people pass the age of 40, they decreasingly feel that they don't make as much as they want. They also feel less capable of change.

Of organizational significance is that the man at age 40 often has too many troubles to be as responsive to the traditional demands of his work organization as he once was. Paradoxically, however, it is at this time that the manager is often in the most important position he will have in his career and in the organization for which he works. Just as the organization is depending most on the individual to make a contribution, his interest in doing so is decreasing. The paradox here is clear and the need for improvement in the situation for the sake of individuals, organizations, and society is apparent.

REDUCING CAREER SUCCESS/ PERSONAL FAILURE

It is now time to turn to an examination of what we can do about the problem of career success and personal failure and the distress it generates. Among the strategies that are available are explicit personal and organizational developmental programs, revised management practices, changed position demands, and restructured life experiences outside the work setting. Although we recognize that no specific technique guarantees success, we are of the belief that various approaches can be developed and implemented which would be of value.

Table 2 outlines a framework for dealing with the problem of management alienation. Obviously, we have not included all the possible techniques that are relevant to this problem. Rather, what we have tried to do is to identify some specific techniques and then structure them into a framework that can be utilized by individuals, organizations, and government agencies seeking to

TABLE TWO

Change Programs for Reducing Management Alienation

I. Organizational programs

    A. Realistic job previews: New managers
                                    Midyear managers

    B. Managerial job restructuring: Increasing planning activities
                                                The mentoring role
                                                Job rotation and team projects

    C. Assessment centers, career counseling, and career development programs

    D. Group training and development programs

    E. Assertiveness training

II. Individual programs

III. Societal/governmental programs

    A. Tax incentives for change programs

    B. Demonstration projects: Funding
                                      Information dissemination
                                      Evaluation

    C. Encouraging societal reeducation

alleviate the management alienation problem. Although it is our opinion that it would be most useful if we were to utilize all the suggestions we have listed, we are realists also. Hence, we urge an implementation of any of the steps outlined, even if the other recommendations are not followed.

In developing our proposals, we have subgrouped them according to organizational, societal and individual recommendations. This is primarily for the sake of convenience, since it is often the case that it is difficult to make clear-cut distinctions among these recommendations in real life.

The possiblity of making a change can be encouraged by the work organization or by society. An individual manager who is interested in a new career can seek a different position in the organization for which he already works (if the organization encourages it) or in a different organization (if society allows it). However, there are, on the other hand, some change programs that are clearly the province of only one entity and of none other (e.g., tax incentives, which can only be changed by the government).

ORGANIZATIONAL PROGRAMS

In this section we begin our discussion of possible change techniques by focusing on those interventions which can be undertaken by the organization. We begin from this vantage point for several reasons. First, we see the organization as a particularly strong influence on the manager because this is the system that has been the major influence on his working life. The organization is important, also, because it has a wide range of techniques available to it and, normally, the resources to use them. In addition, since the organization has a great need to resolve the difficulties we have described, we can expect a willingness on its part to undertake appropriate programs.

Realistic Job Previews

Cambridge, Mass.—Svea Fraser never had any doubts about her husband's ultimate business success. Her fears were of a different order.

"I was concerned at what would happen to us, earning a good deal of money," said Mrs. Fraser, a 29-year-old psychology graduate and a former Peace Corps worker. "I was afraid of success. I was afraid it would grab me."

Over the last few months, her fears have dissipated, if not evaporated. Mrs. Fraser and 21 other women have been accompanying their husbands to a weekly class on "The Executive Family" offered to second-year students at the Harvard Business School. There are also two husbands in the class, accompanying wives who are business school students.

"I was delighted that someone shared my concern at what can happen to a successful family," said Mrs. Fraser, the mother of a 2½-year-old daughter. "It may sound strange but it was a relief to know that there is something to be afraid of . . . that it isn't just an imagined fear."

Bypass Personal Details

To Dr. Barrie Greiff, the psychiatrist who originated the course in 1970 and still conducts it, the fears of executive families are well founded. His experience with "talented, aggressive people" had shown him that executives who planned business strategies down to the last detail often believed that their marriage and personal lives would take care of themselves.

He set about designing a course that would encourage couples to "creatively think about creatively designing their lives," a course that would not provide pat answers, but would act as catalyst and challenge its participants.

"Nobody in America would challenge the idea of families, but what happens is that people take marriage and families for granted," Dr. Greiff noted. "I think business is concerned with profits. It's not business's responsibility to worry about families. It's the individual's responsibility to look at his or her life."

Dr. Greiff's course, 16 weekly classes of about two hours each, is confined to 25 couples (one spouse must be a second-year business school student). There is a wide variation in age, background and previous business experience, a fact made possible because there are almost three applicants for each class opening.

Problems Are Listed

Dr. Greiff, who spent two years in the Navy and two years studying psychiatry at Harvard before joining the staff in 1968, centers discussions on problems most likely to be encountered by upwardly mobile couples.

Among them are the possible conflict of dual careers in a family, the question of priorities in business and personal life, the trauma of divorce or job loss, the question of whether or not to have children, difficulties encountered in relocating, and problems engendered by a spouse who is constantly traveling.

"This is not direct therapy... it isn't for fractured marriages," said Dr. Greiff, who has a wife with a career of her own.

"The course is valuable because it gives people options to think about. There is always a conflict between personal needs... and a corporation's needs. The individual must create a mechanism that allows him to participate in a little of each.

"It may mean giving up some goals and aspirations. It may mean talking to one's employer. It may mean quitting and taking another job. People have to clearly think what their priorities are, and what their tradeoffs are."

The tradeoff for Svea and Scott Fraser came earlier than most. Mr. Fraser, a 29-year-old former navy lieutenant and intelligence officer who later spent two years with the Defense Intelligence Agency was recently offered a job as general manager of a Saudi Arabian company he is helping to set up. It involved living abroad for a year, without his wife and child.

"I made up my mind to give up the general managership to spend the first year working in the operation in Boston," he said. "In essence it was the job versus the family, and it was a tough decision. It was a wrenching experience for me because the business was something our group was creating and it was the fulfillment of a dream."

Mr. Fraser, who registered for the course because he appreciated that his wife would also be involved, attributed his decision to "facing things through, as a result of Dr. Greiff's course."

"It was such a liberating experience being able to give up that general manager job," he said. "I thought I'd wake up and feel bad but I didn't. I felt great. It's the first time I've ever had a perspective on myself."

Source: Enid Nemy. Couples take a course to avoid the dangers of success, *New York Times*, April 26, 1976, p. 44.

This passage from an article in the *New York Times* illustrates one of the most effective ways to reduce management alienation, a technique that has come to be known as the *realistic job preview* (RJP). It is an approach based on research findings and is designed to reduce the disconfirmed expectancies we have seen as so important. The RJP involves preparing individuals for their future careers by giving them as much information as possible regarding what their future is likely to be, both *good* and *bad,* as opposed to stressing the positive only, as is frequently the case either intentionally or unintentionally.

The course taken at the Harvard Business School illustrates the concept of the RJP quite well. As the excerpt indicates, a realistic perspective on the managerial career is developed, including both positives and negatives. This helps future executives and their spouses to realize more fully the nature of the choices they are about to make and the inevitable positive and negative outcomes that are always involved in these, or any, choices.

Another approach to realistic job previews is the technique of developing accurate descriptions of *what a manager actually does* in his everyday job activities and then communicating this information to individuals and organizations when career decisions are being made. It is possible to use this technique early in a person's career, when initial decisions are being made, or later on, when midcareer changes are being considered. In Table 3 we present, in this job description, some of the types of managerial tasks that we have found to be often descriptive of managers' jobs in various combinations.

While useful as descriptions of management jobs we do not claim these factors to be descriptive of this or any other management job in their full complexity. It is our experience, however,

TABLE THREE

Position: Product Manager

Section A: Position requirements and goals

1. Develop plan for long-range product and market growth.
2. Develop marketing systems and procedures.
3. Create new products.
4. Evaluate new plans and products according to "bottom line" demands.
5. Develop promotion ideas.

Section B: Critical skills and abilities

	Ranking of importance for position
1. *Skill in oral communications* (the ability to engage effectively and communicate desires and expectations to individuals or a group)	7
2. *Skill in written communications* (the ability to present ideas and perspectives effectively through written reports, presentations, and memoranda)	6

3. *Skill in human relations* (the ability to empathize with others, to understand their needs, and to translate this understanding into effective work behavior) 5
4. *Persuasive skills* (the ability to project one's point of view and desires to others and to convince them of their desirability) 3.5
5. *Creativity* (the ability to develop and accept new ideas, new products, and new procedures for meeting work goals) 1.5
6. *Objectivity* (*willingness to accept criticism*) (the capability for being nondefensive and for accepting strengths and weaknesses) 3.5
7. *Flexibility* (the capability for changing behavior according to changing situational requirements) 8
8. *Tolerance of uncertainty* (the ability to operate effectively in situations without clear guidelines and with incomplete information) 9
9. *Resistance to stress* (the capability for operating effectively in situations of extreme demands, high tension, and high anxiety) 10
10. *Planning skills* (the ability to organize the work requirements and to structure activities so as to maximize the likelihood of goal attainment) 1.5

Section C: Critical position demands

Rating of position's critical demands[a]

I. *Integration and coordination:* This activity involves coordinating and directing the efforts of different groups with different priorities and values toward a common goal. 3.3
II. *Short-range problem-solving:* This task involves responding to and resolving problems which are not

---

[a] A rating of 4 or higher indicates that the demand was rated as key for the position; a rating of 3–3.9 indicates that the demand was rated as of moderate importance for the position; a rating of 2.9 or below indicates that the demand was rated as of little importance for the position.

expected and for which routine procedures and guidelines do not exist. 2.7

III. *Internal consulting:* This activity involves providing special technical expertise and knowledge to the demands which other managers encounter. It also requires the person to keep abreast of and to increase his knowledge in the areas of specialization. 5.0

IV. *Stimulating company growth:* This activity involves seeking possibilities and mechanisms for company growth by being sensitive to and assessing the attitudes and needs of customers and by planning for new, while improving old, products and markets. 5.0

V. *Leadership and supervision:* This task involves assuming responsibility for the traditional tasks of motivating and leading subordinates. 1.0

VI. *Consumer responsibilities:* This task involves monitoring and attending to the needs of customers. It also involves negotiating with customers when this is appropriate. 5.0

VII. *Financial management:* This activity involves monitoring worker and company activities according to financial criteria, making decisions according to these considerations, and evaluating alternatives according to their financial implications. 4.8

VIII. *Personnel development:* This activity involves training and developing new and existing employees. It may also involve recruiting, interviewing, and selecting personnel. 2.2

IX. *Community affairs:* This involves engaging in tasks designed to enhance the public image of the company's products and services. 1.0

X. *Long-range planning:* This task involves being concerned with the long-range future of the company and planning appropriately for it. 4.8

that describing management jobs according to these factors has enabled us to gain a realistic picture of various management postions. This picture then becomes utilizable when we attempt to help executives or managers thinking of making career changes. Their use enables us to point out to potential controllers that the position often involves more personnel activities than they may have thought and also a considerable amount of internal consulting. On the other hand, the potential marketing manager will often need to be less concerned with leadership and supervision than he may have thought.

It is because of this practical, functional experience and the research-established fruitfulness of RJPs that we recommend the use of the types of job descriptive information presented in Table 3 in counseling managers and potential managers about the kinds of jobs they may be applying for and are considering entering. Showing how different jobs are either high or low on these different factors provides the types of realistic job previews that help reduce the management alienation that is the subject of this book.

MANAGERIAL JOB RESTRUCTURING

There is another way that a knowledge of job characteristics can be useful in reducing management alienation and that is to change the job to fit the man rather than move the man to fit the job. This approach, very popular today for blue- and white-collar operative positions, has rarely been used with managers, although there is no reason that it cannot be. The advantage would be that we would then have a mechanism for decreasing management alienation through appropriate job design, regardless of who is occupying the position at the time. Hence, it provides us an opportunity for improvement without having to deal with such problems as recommending a job change which may not be desired and/or selecting new individuals for particular positions with all the difficulties this entails.

The factors we have listed in Table 3 for describing management jobs can be useful in achieving this goal. Suppose that a management job was changed to include more of factor X (long-range planning). Based on our previous argument, we would predict that this would result in less alienation, since these individuals would feel they were now more in control of their own fate and less controlled by others. In research we have conducted with Dorothy Lang of Baruch College, these are the results we have obtained.

There are other ways of restructuring management jobs. One way is to have the management job satisfy what the noted psychoanalyst Erik Erikson has called the increased interest in "mentoring" among men entering into and going through their middle years. This process, which fits in nicely with what we have described as the *personnel development* factor in Table 3, describes the increased desire of men at this age to pass on their experiences and their knowledge to the upcoming generation. In particular, the desire often is to pass on knowledge and experience in areas and matters not easily taught by other methods.

We think that this characteristic of men at this age could be utilized very meaningfully in restructuring the management position to the benefit of both individuals and their work organizations. The reason is that there are several factors involved in many management jobs which are not easily learned except by experience in the particular organization one is working for.

Of significance here are the management demands in Table 3 we have called *integration and coordination* (factor I) and *internal consulting* (factor III). Each of these involves wide-reaching interpersonal skills which depend for their effectiveness primarily on a knowledge of the culture and history of the organization in which one is working. An experienced manager passing on his skills and knowledge in this area as part of his regular job duties would be of great value.

The experienced manager acting as a "mentor" could pass on his knowledge to younger managers in other ways besides these. To illustrate, he can discuss with the younger managers how he has personally dealt with such typical managerial demands as:

1. Fulfilling the job of evaluating others.
2. Handling common personal problems (e.g., mobility, the conflicts between career and family, etc.).

3. Meeting the task of discharging others when it is necessary.

The management job can be restructured in other ways besides the introduction of increased "mentoring" activities. We have already suggested that managerial positions can be changed to allow increased autonomy. Another possibility for changing the job is to increase the feedback the individual manager gets from his work. This is an important factor which is often ignored. One way to do this is to increase the frequency and adequacy of performance appraisals. However, other possibilities may be looked into so that the manager will know how he is doing. (We will discuss this further in the next section.) It is also possible, even without a formal job change, to increase the variety of tasks assigned to him, their significance, and their uniqueness.

One note of caution. We are not suggesting that these job changes always work. Sometimes, if the changes are not prepared for properly or if the new tasks are not rewarded appropriately by the organization, they will fail. The point is they *can* succeed because they involve changes in task and social activity and thus are of value in reducing one's sense of personal and social alienation.

Assessment Centers, Career Counseling, and Career Development Programs

We pointed out earlier that one of the real needs of managers in organizations is to reduce the sense of anonymity they feel; that is, the feeling that nobody knows who they are, what their characteristic strengths and weaknesses are, and what their desires for the future are. As a result of this feeling, there is an increased tendency to believe that one is powerless in the grip of some noncontrollable force which is external to oneself and which has little concern for one as an individual. This sense of powerlessness generates a feeling that one will not be able to implement one's needs in the future. It also makes it impossible to understand the needs of others who are also being controlled by that same external force. When everyone is being controlled by and will continue to be controlled by the same external mechanism, the result is a feeling of high personal and social alienation.

One way in which this sense of estrangement can be reduced is for the organization to institute meaningful, comprehensive assessments of its managerial personnel and to develop and implement career counseling/career development programs which utilize these assessments in conjunction with organizational needs.

Assessment centers are not new; we have had them in this country for 40 years and they were established in Germany even earlier. However, their application to managers and executives really dates from the mid-50s when the American Telephone and Telegraph Company began to bring together groups of managers who had been cited by their supervisors as having significant managerial potential. Once brought together in a particular setting, they were "assessed" for their potential within the AT&T organization. They were observed in group discussions and simulation exercises by senior company executives and professional human resource personnel and administered a variety of self-report questionnaires and psychological measures of abilities, attitudes, and personality. All of this information, which generally took several days to gather, was then used as a basis for making judgments about each individual on a variety of dimensions thought to be important for success at AT&T. To illustrate, the traditional dimensions of evaluation that have been used by the AT&T assessors are:

1. Scholastic aptitude
2. Oral and written communication skills
3. Human relations skills
4. Personal impact
5. Perception of threshold social cues
6. Creativity

7. Self-objectivity
8. Social objectivity
9. Behavior flexibility
10. Need approval of superiors
11. Need approval of peers
12. Inner work standards
13. Need achievement
14. Need security
15. Goal flexibility
16. Primacy of work
17. Bell System value orientation
18. Realism of expectations
19. Tolerance of uncertainty
20. Ability to delay gratification
21. Resistance to stress
22. Range of interests
23. Energy
24. Organization and planning
25. Decision making

Unfortunately, for our purposes, the early AT&T centers did not make the results of the assessments available to either the individuals involved or to company representatives. This was because the original emphasis of the centers was on predicting success within AT&T. Their purpose was to identify those individuals who would eventually become the better executives. Had these evaluations been made available to each assessee, a value of a different kind would have been achieved. Each manager would have been provided information that would have been of great value in helping him plan his career activities to meet his personal needs. He would have received a clear picture of his strengths and weaknesses and his characteristics as seen by others. It would also have provided him with a clear picture of his position in the organization and given him the knowledge he needed to plan a career of reduced personal and social alienation. Such knowledge and information about oneself and one's place in the organization can, in and of itself, reduce one's immediate sense of alienation, even without the formal career development programs we will discuss below.

Assessment centers vary greatly between different companies according to such factors as the types of measures used, the length of the assessment, the number of assessors, and the location of the assessments. Although it is not clear whether these particular variations make any real difference in their effectiveness, one recent innovation, also taking place at AT&T, is of importance for use here. This is their midcareer assessment center for managers. Instead of the traditional focus on young managers with most of their careers ahead of them, this particular program is geared to the middle-aged manager and his problems. In these centers feedback is being provided to the participants with the intention of aiding them in their self-clarification as individuals and in their roles as managers with years of contribution ahead in the AT&T organization. This newer program supports one of the major premises underlying this book (i.e., the manager is a different person at midlife than he was fifteen years earlier). Thus, while the manager at the midcareer center is assessed on the types of traditional dimensions we have outlined above, he is also assessed at this time on factors more relevant to his current stage of life. Among these are such questions as:

1. Will his job performance and commitment to the company change between now and retirement?
2. Will he retire early (before age 65)?
3. How will he adjust to retirement?
4. How satisfied with his career will he feel when it is over?
5. How satisfied with his life will he feel when he reaches old age?
6. Will he experience a critical disturbance in his personal adjustment between now and retirement?

AT&T is still working on the development and effective utilization of its midcareer assessment center and it is by no means as well structured as it will be in the coming years. We would expect, however, that as this articulation takes place, one of its most important beneficial effects will be the impact it has on reducing the sense of alienation experienced by managers.

In summary, one of the important ways to reduce management alienation is for the manager to know that he is being assessed clearly, regularly, objectively, and impartially. This reduces his sense of helplessness at being at the mercy of unknown, massive, external forces. We believe, however, that this is only a first step. Assessments need to be communicated to the individual and he also needs to receive guidance in interpreting these assessments in light of organizational needs and his career possibilities within the organization, both present and future. Assessments of individuals are necessary and desirable in reducing alienation, but they do not reach their full potential unless they are integrated into and utilized in conjunction with an overall career development program.

The typical career development program has several components. First, it takes an inventory of the individual manager's capabilities and weaknesses. This usually consists of information from tests of abilities, interests, and capabilities, and of the results of performance appraisals performed in the organization. These two sets of information give the necessary picture of a manager's potential (i.e. the test information) and his current performance. These data are then integrated with the requirements of those organizational positions for which the individual may be considered a possibility and with information about current and projected openings. Combining this profile of the individual with knowledge of real corporate opportunities provides guidelines for the individual to choose and enter those positions which will be most personally satisfying to him, while simultaneously taking account of organizational realities.

To be more specific, setting up a career development program begins by obtaining answers to the following questions:

1. What kinds of work interests does an individual manager have? What kinds of abilities and skills? (This can be obtained by psychological testing.)
2. What types and levels of work capabilities is he currently exhibiting? (This can be obtained by organizational performance appraisals.)
3. What are the explicit role demands of different jobs in the organization? (This can be obtained by determining how the jobs rate on the task demand factors listed in Table 3.)
4. How many job openings will be available in the different career fields in the organization in the next five years? ten years?

A career plan based on an individual's interests and capabilities, job demands, and predicted job openings can then be made and implemented. The way in which this might be done is as follows:

Step 1: The individual manager engages in a self-assessment and makes exploratory choices about his career. In making these choices he uses each of the units of information mentioned above.

Step 2: The manager has a career development conference with appropriate corporate personnel. The topics to be discussed are the self-assessments and the choices he made in Step 1 and how these jibe with the kinds of choices the organization might feel appropriate for him.

Step 3: The manager and the corporate representative then formulate a career plan for the individual. Among the possible decisions they might come to, based on Steps 1 and 2, are such alternatives as (a) more intensive training for a current position; (b) retraining for a new position; (c) geographic mobility for personal reasons; (d) horizontal mobility with no change in job level; or (e) a restructuring, with new responsibilities, of the manager's current position.

FIGURE 7
Sample Presentation of Information Input for Career Development Planning

Career Development Information

Critical behavior demands	(1) You have rated yourself as being interested in these job demands as follows:	(2) You have been rated by your supervisor as to degree of competence in these job demands as follows:	(3)	(4)	(5)	(6)
			Column (3) indicates the critical job demands of your current position; columns (4), (5) and (6) indicate the critical demands of those positions—careers you have expressed some interest in:			
I. *Integration:* This activity involves coordinating and directing the efforts of different groups with different priorities and values toward a common goal.	4	3	5	2	5	1
II. *Marketing and Customer Service:* This activity involves monitoring and attending to the needs of customers. This also involves interpreting those needs for the purpose of product and market planning.	1	3	1	4	3	3
X. *Long-Range Planning:* This activity involves being concerned with the long-range future of the company and planning appropriately for it.	3	2	1	2	4	5

Figure 7 illustrates how the specific types of information we have cited as being relevant can be combined with one another and presented to an individual manager within the context of an overall management and career development program. As you can see, the manager is presented with a description of his likes and dislikes, his supervisors' appraisal of him, and the demands of the different positions available to him in the organization. The particular manager involved would then use this information in the discussions he has with the company representative relative to his career opportunities in that organization.

Group Training-Development Programs

> At the fifth meeting the group's feeling about its own progress became the initial focus of discussion. The "talkers" participated as usual, conversation shifting rapidly from one point to another. Dissatisfaction was mounting, expressed through loud, snide remarks by some and through apathy by others.
>
> George Franklin appeared partcularly disturbed. Finally pounding the table, he exclaimed, "I don't know what is going on here! I should be paid for listening to this drivel! I'm getting just a bit sick of wasting my time here. If the profs don't put out—I quit!" George was pleased; he was angry, and he said so. As he sat back in his chair, he felt he had the group behind him. He felt he had the guts to say what most of the others were thinking! Some members of the group applauded loudly, but others showed obvious disapproval. They wondered why George was excited over so insignificant an issue, why he hadn't done something constructive rather than just sounding off as usual. Why, they wondered, did he say their comments were "drivel?"
>
> George Franklin became the focus of discussion. "What do you mean, George, by saying this is nonsense?" "What do you expect, a neat set of rules to meet all your problems?"
>
> George was getting uncomfortable. These were questions

difficult for him to answer. Gradually he began to realize that a large part of the group disagreed with him; then he began to wonder why. He was learning something about people he hadn't known before. ... "How does it feel, George, to have people disagree with you when you thought you had them behind you ... ?"

Bob White was first annoyed with George and now with the discussion. He was getting tense, a bit shaky, perhaps. Bob didn't like anybody to get a raw deal, and he felt that George was getting it. At first Bob tried to minimize George's outburst, and then he suggested that the group get on to the real issues; but the group continued to focus on George. Finally, Bob said, "Why don't you leave George alone and stop picking on him? We're not getting anywhere this way."

With the help of the leaders, the group focused on Bob. "What do you mean, 'picking' on him? Why, Bob, have you tried to change the discussion? Why are you so protective of George?" Bob began to realize that the group wanted to focus on George; he also saw that George didn't think he was being picked on, but felt he was learning something about himself and how others reacted to him. "Why do I always get upset," Bob began to wonder, "when people get angry at each other?" ... Now Bob was learning something about how people saw him while gaining some insight into his own behavior.

Source: R. Tannenbaum, I. Wechsler, and F. Massarik, *Leadership and Organization: A Behavioral Science Approach* (New York: McGraw-Hill Book Company, 1961), p. 123; used with permission of the publisher.

The kinds of attitudinal change that we see being elicited in George and Bob in this description of what takes place in a group training-development program illustrates why we view this technique as potentially one of the major tools for the reduction of management alienation.

Group training tries to reduce personal and social alienation by encouraging trainees to open up about their fears, their anxieties, and their real selves. In this way, the individual learns about himself and other people and how we develop and maintain our social relationships. One way that group training helps us learn about ourselves is that it stresses minimizing or eliminating hierarchical distinctions between people. In addition, attention is focused on the here-and-now (i.e., the behavior taking place at the time) rather than on the previous thoughts and classifications of the people involved. Thus, training groups examine how individuals react to one another and how and why they do or do not combine to form groups. Throughout the process individuals are encouraged to be honest with each other and themselves, although this may be uncomfortable, and also to express hostility and feelings of dejection and frustration when these are warranted. As a result, group sessions can get stormy, but the idea is that you cannot really learn about (and accept) yourself and others unless there is openness and honesty.

Why doesn't the group break up? Ideally, the reason is that the experience is nonevaluative and has a climate of psychological safety. Another key is that the leader also needs to be honest and open about himself and others, to accept negative comments directed at him by others, to give others honest feedback, and to be nonevaluative. The more he does this, the more the rest of the group will achieve the goal of getting in touch with themselves and others and exhibit their own fears and anxieties without the added fear of being attacked by others.

The Johari window, an idea suggested by Luft,[31] is one technique for opening up group participants and encouraging self-realization. The window is actually a four-cell table for classifying the kinds of knowledge we know and do not know. It looks like this:

		Feedback from Others	
		Known to self	Unknown to self
Disclosures by the Self	Known to others	Public Area	Blind Area
	Unknown to others	Hidden Area	Unknown Area

The Johari window enables us to classify a person who is highly anxious but who appears cool to others as *hidden*. Similarly, a person who is obnoxious to others but doesn't know it is *blind*. The idea of group-development training is to decrease both of these situations and to move the individual toward the *public* area by giving him knowledge of how he is perceived and comes across to others. By encouraging him to open up more about himself to others (reducing his *hidden* area) and to himself (reducing his *blind* area), he is able to achieve a reduced sense of social alienation from others and a reduced sense of personal alienation from himself.

Group training also encourages an individual to accept and try out different roles without waiting for them to be assigned. Practicing these roles gives the individual greater insight into his own attitudes and into his attitudes toward others, thus reducing his sense of personal and social alienation in a manner that might be very difficult to achieve if we only looked at people from the outside.

Group development training also focuses on people as people and what we learn about each other from experiencing life together. It rejects the notion of describing people according to their demographic characteristics or their statistical properties. We learn about people and ourselves and become less alienated from them and ourselves by sharing experiences with one another, rather than by studying the properties of the categories to which we are assigned or assign ourselves. This commonality of experience makes our interactions more human, richer, and less alienating than if the communication took place along solely rational, technological, and conceptual grounds.

Another proposed advantage of group training is that the sharing of experience enables a greater growth of the individuals involved in the sense that they come to learn more about their capabilities and competencies. Hence, they learn more about what they can do themselves and they learn to rely less on technology and rationality as mechanisms for influencing events and people. To many people, including us, this is, theoretically, a valuable corrective to our overly impersonal, technological society and the alienation it sometimes stimulates.

Does group training work? Does its emphasis on *you can do it yourself,* personal control and *life is what you make of it* reduce personal alienation and estrangement from others? If we disentangle ourselves from the polemics that group training has generated over the past several decades, a fairly impartial conclusion would be that the proponents of group training are correct when they say it has positive effects, *at least some of the time.* Trainees do often become more aware of their personal needs and they do often become less estranged from others. However, there are at least three limitations to this positive conclusion. First, the positive effects do not always occur. Second, the effects may wear off over time. Third, it may be that a particular organization is not interested in reducing management alienation, despite the benefits to be derived, and will discourage the implementation or expression of such changes, even *when it would be better for the organization* for them to take place.

There are a number of factors that can increase the likelihood that individuals who have attended a group training program and have had their personal and social alienation reduced will be able to apply their new skills for the benefit of the organization. First, the organization itself must become more supportive of the principles of group training. One way to do this is to utilize a version of the Realistic Job Preview technique we discussed earlier. Consider the following examples of what takes place in these group training and development programs:

> Expression of negative feelings.
> Description of past feelings.
> Expression and exploration of personally meaningful material.
> Expression of interpersonal emotions to others in group.
> Provision of feedback to others as to their personal expressions and feelings.

Confrontation of others about their feelings.
Assistance to others to articulate their interpersonal concerns.
Expression of positive feelings and closeness to others.

Since these processes are generally part of group training sessions, an organization's readiness to accept them can be increased by first advising the potential trainees of what will take place. Their reactions will indicate how ready they are for group training. They will also be provided with a realistic job preview (of a type) which can decrease the likelihood of distress and withdrawal once they are in the training. Finally, the material can also be distributed to others in the organization who are not participating in the training. Such exposure has the advantage of enabling the nonparticipants to better understand the attitudes and behaviors of those returning from the training.

The likelihood of the program being accepted can be further increased by doing a diagnostic analysis of the organization and then deciding whether to go ahead based on the results. Such questions as the following can be asked:

1. How much does the organization support the principle of self-actualization?
2. Do the key people in the organization support the training?
3. Are the people who want the training and/or who will conduct it reasonably secure in their jobs?
4. Does the organization feel that interpersonal change is legitimate?
5. Are the goals of the program well understood?

Unless there is a yes answer to all or most of these questions, there will be little reason to go ahead. Group training will not be fruitful, regardless of the alienation levels of the managers in the organization, regardless of the program's potential utility and regardless of the objective problems of the organization.

A few further points. Group training, to be of use to both the individual and the organization, should not, in the process of encouraging emotional openness, deprecate rationality and intellectuality. It should not arouse an elite feeling among the participants, a process that would inevitably lead to divisiveness and intergroup conflict. Most organizations already have too much of this. Also, group training should not foster an undervaluing of individuality as individuals come to see the nature of interpersonal, group-oriented processes. All of these are problems that can occur, but they do not have to and they will not if the program is well thought out and developed.

The final major problem is the kinds of people who will attend. No training group will be successful unless it has participants who are willing to engage in the activities and who do not have a strong emotional repugnance toward discussing their interpersonal problems and themselves. It is a waste of time for resistant people to attend, except under the most unusual circumstances. The problem for us to be aware of is that when we refer to organizational managers, we are often referring to individuals who have been raised in a traditional male ethic and who may often fall into this category of "not likely to be easily accepting of group training." This is a problem that needs to be dealt with if we are going to use group-training techniques to reduce management alienation. We believe that changing cultural norms are helping greatly in this process and that this will accelerate in the future assisted by the acceptance of and recognition by many managers of their own alienation and distress.

Assertiveness Training: Accepting Yourself and Accepting Others

You have the right to:

1. Judge your own behavior, thoughts, and emotions, and to take the responsibility for their initiation and consequences upon yourself.

2. Offer no reasons or excuses justifying your behavior.
havior.
3. Judge whether you are responsible for finding solutions to other people's problems.
4. Change your mind.
5. Make mistakes—and be responsible for them.
6. Say, "I don't know."
7. Be independent of the goodwill of others before coping with them.
8. Be illogical in making decisions.
9. Say, "I don't understand."
10. Say, "I don't care."

This statement of human rights has come to be prominently associated with assertiveness training, a technique that seeks to have the participant accept the fact that he is not perfect, not always strong, not always able to meet norms, and that he is what he is and others are what they are. This acceptance of the self and of others, if achieved, clearly marks this type of training program as a potentially useful mechanism for reducing personal and social alienation among managers.

Assertiveness training sessions generally start by stressing the human rights we have outlined here. If people learn how to assert these rights in normal, everyday interactions, they will come to understand themselves and be more in touch with their feelings and personal needs, and others will be more in touch with them and understand them. It should be noted, however, that not all of these rights are equally applicable in the work setting. People cannot work cooperatively, as they must at work, without some underlying rationality. In other words, one cannot just say, "I can ignore you and do whatever I want without offering excuses" and still expect to work effectively with other people. We would therefore suggest that rights 2 and 8 can be implemented by managers in their work roles only to a modest degree. We would not overstate these limitations, however. There is a certain attitude about yourself and others that is being proposed here. It is an attitude that you can accept and be in touch with yourself and others although neither one of you is perfect in a societal sense. Your characteristics are you, and you don't have to hide from yourself and others.

How do you come to learn and accept these personal characteristics and those of others? Some of the techniques of assertiveness training are:

1. *Broken record:* This involves training an individual to repeat to himself, over and over again, his particular wants and desires (i.e., those needs that are very much his). This enables that person to learn his own particular need structure and to accept it without being emotional and/or defensive about it.

2. *Fogging:* This involves learning to accept criticisms, even when they may be manipulative, while always reserving the right to make one's own personal judgments, imperfect though they may be. This skill opens the person more to himself by enabling him to become less defensive about himself (since he is accepting the legitimacy of criticism) and less anxious about being perfect. At the same time, he is also accepting himself more by not allowing himself to be influenced by those who are trying to manipulate him.

3. *Negative assertion:* This carries the *fogging* concept even further by teaching an acceptance of personal faults through agreeing with criticism from others, whether constructive or hostile. At the same time, the individual is taught not to apologize for his imperfections.

4. *Free information:* This involves learning to recognize the social cues given off by others. The effect, when learned, is a reduction of social alienation.

5. *Negative inquiry:* This involves learning how to prompt criticism from others in order to acquire useful information about the self or to show others how they are being

manipulative. The value is that it encourages the individual to accept the self more by being less anxious to learn about the self and it also helps relationships with others more by helping these others to see where they are being manipulative. A decreased personal and social alienation occurs as a result of both processes.

6. *Self-disclosure:* This involves learning how to initiate discussions about one's characteristics, both positive and negative. It reduces personal alienation by encouraging a person to learn and discuss one's own personal characteristics and it reduces social alienation by enhancing the ability of the learner to communicate with others and understand them better.

7. *Workable compromise:* This involves beginning to come to grips with and accepting what is crucial to the self and what is not. It enables the learner to learn how to compromise about noncrucial matters and how not to compromise about those matters which are of crucial importance to one's sense of self.

The following excerpt is an illustration of assertiveness training, how it affects the individuals involved, and why it can be of value in dealing with the alienation problem.

At the time of this dialogue, I was consulting for a drama study group that included Carl, a former Broadway musical star, and other young actors and actresses whose faces were so familiar from their TV commercials but had no names to go with them. I was consulting on how to be systematically assertive to casting directors, reading committees, directors, production assistants, producers and the whole lot of fringe "backers," "experts," "critics," and "gofers" that the actor must cope with. Carl brought up a problem of being pressured and manipulated by the producer of a film soon to go into production. Carl's agent has two possible contracted roles in negotiation, one of them with this producer. His agent may recommend that he take one over the other, neither, or even both if scheduling commitments could be worked out. The producer, on the other hand, wanted Carl to sign a production contract with him immediately. Carl's agent meanwhile was negotiating on the second possible role. Carl did not want to tell the producer that he was considering another role in place of the one being offered for fear that he would lose the producer's goodwill on future negotiations or that the producer would use this information to foul up the negotiations on the other contract. In short, Carl had a problem in communicating his desire not to make a commitment immediately and to negotiate a commitment time limit sufficient to decide which role to contract for. Carl had had an encounter with the producer shortly before the consultation with me; he had begged off giving his decision but had promised to see him as soon as possible. The following coached dialogue was set up in the drama group to allow Carl to practice being systematically assertive in avoiding a premature commitment without being rude, short, apologetic, or making the producer angry or insulting him. Although the setting of this situation dialogue is the exotic cinematographic production business, systematically asserting oneself to one's present or future employer to avoid a manipulated commitment is equally applicable in almost all other life occupations.

Setting of the dialogue: Carl is seated in Mr. Mogul's office as the producer breezes through the waiting room, greets Carl, and whisks him into his inner office.

Producer: Carl, this is the role for you. If this doesn't make it for you, nothing will. I've just come from upstairs and everybody is really enthusiastic over you playing the role of Marvin.

Carl: That's great. I agree with them. I think I could do a good job on it too. (*Fogging*)

Producer: Fabulous! All we need is the contract signed and we'll have a drink on it.

Carl: Great! I'll have the drink if I sign, but I still want some time to decide. (*Self-disclosure*)

Producer: What do you need time for? It's a great part and the money's good. Hal thinks so too. He's your agent and he negotiated the terms.

Carl: I agree, but I don't want to make a commitment yet. *(Fogging* and *Broken record)*

Producer: Carl, we really want you on this production. I've worked hard upstairs to get the rest of the staff enthusiastic for you. We all want you now. Don't let me down after all the trouble I went to for you.

Carl: I hope I don't disappoint you, Sol, but I still don't want to make a commitment right now. *(Self-disclosure* and *Broken record)*

Producer: We leave for location in two weeks. We need a commitment right now. Don't pass up this part, Carl.

Carl: You're probably right, Sol, so how long can you give me to decide? *(Fogging* and *Workable compromise)*

Producer: I'll need your signature by tomorrow.

Carl: I'm sure you do, Sol, but that's not enough time for me. How about it if I let you know before you leave for location? That's two weeks. That should be enough time for me to decide. *(Fogging* and *Workable compromise)*

Producer: Carl! We can't do that. We'd have to break off production and come back here to get a replacement if you said no; screw up the whole schedule!

Carl: I don't understand. Don't you have a second choice picked out? *(Self-disclosure)*

Producer: Not yet. We haven't found anyone near you for this part. If you don't sign, Carl, you'll be missing a great role.

Carl: You're probably right, Sol, but I still want some time to decide. Let's look at the calendar. You leave on the twenty-eighth, right? I'll give you my decision on the twenty-third. That would give you five working days to find someone else, if I say no. How's that sound? *(Fogging, Broken record,* and *Workable compromise)*

Producer: That's cutting it very close for me, Carl.

Carl: I'm sure it is, Sol, but I need time and you need time. This gives us both some leeway. (*Fogging, Broken Record,* and *Workable Compromise*)

Producer: You give me no choice. What way is that to be after all I've done for you?

Carl: You're right, Sol, it's a hell of a way to operate. I wish I could let you know that I would sign, but I'm not going to make a commitment right now (*Fogging, Self-disclosure,* and *Broken record*)

Producer: If you decide earlier, you will let me know right away?

Carl: Of course I will, Sol. As soon as I decide (*Workable compromise*)

Producer: We're counting on you for this part.

Carl; I know you are, Sol, and I want to take it, but I just need more time. (*Self-disclosure* and *Broken record*)

Source: M. J. Smith, *When I Say No, I Feel Guilty* (New York: The Dial Press, 1975), pp. 185–188.

INDIVIDUAL PROGRAMS

We have been discussing what an organization can do to deal with career success and personal failure among its managers. We now turn to the steps an individual can take on his own if he finds himself in this situation and wants to get out.

Clearly, one does not need to wait for the company for which one works to establish programs in assertiveness training and group development aimed at personal growth. Nor does one need to limit oneself to company-sponsored programs, even when they do exist. Programs of the kind we have described here are gaining in popularity today, and the individual wishing to enter such a program will have little trouble finding proffered aid.

His dilemma will be more in deciding whether he should focus on organizational training and growth programs, focus more on a personal therapy alternative, or undertake some type of an integrated program for change. We have no particular recommendation to make here except to note the obvious complexity of the situation and the frequent need for professional help in making a decision.

One step the individual can take to make it more likely that any developmental program that he enters will be helpful is to undertake as complete an assessment of himself as possible. This means that he would have to overlook the (often exaggerated) personal threats it may pose. Such assessments are available in professional offices, local agencies, and university counseling centers. These assessments are of value not only for the individual thinking of entering personal development programs of either an individual or group nature, but can also help the individual thinking of career changes, educational programs and even residential moves. All choices of this type need accurate assessments of the individuals involved. A personally undertaken assessment gives that.

Perhaps what is most important, however, for the individual in the career success/personal failure situation is that he needs to understand and undertake a radical restructuring of his thinking processes. Most specifically, he needs to understand that he *can change* his life situation and that he does not need to remain where he is, although until now he has devoted his working life to that career and life-style. It is also the area in which people most frequently need professional help. Recognizing the possibility of change increases the likelihood of a successful resolution of the career success/personal failure dilemma. Yet it is often the most difficult to achieve because of the investments that have been made in career and life-style and the resultant costs of change.

The key, we believe, is for the individual to accept two considerations:

1. Financial costs are often cheaper than psychological costs.

2. A change, when planned for and not entered into precipitously, can often cost less in both financial and psychological costs than originally estimated.

One further point is that the individual in the career success/personal failure life situation should start thinking of himself both as an individual and as a person with a network of ties to others who are all affected by his decision. Please note that we are not suggesting that the individual should focus only on his responsibility to himself and ignore the needs of others. Far from it. Rather, what we are suggesting is that recognition of one's personal needs, in addition to the needs of others with whom one is linked, are *both* essential ingredients of developing a more effective life situation.

SOCIETAL/GOVERNMENTAL PROGRAMS

We have emphasized throughout this book the importance to society in general of the career success/personal failure problem. It is because of this significance that we think there is a role for governmental institutions to play here. (In making these recommendations we take no position on the appropriate size of government. This is a matter for discussion elsewhere. Rather, our assumption is that government will continue to operate at current levels for the foreseeable future. Hence, we believe they have a role to play.) This role, we believe, can be outlined as follows:

1. The government should provide tax and financial incentives designed to encourage intra- and multiorganizational programs aimed at reducing the career success/personal failure syndrome.
2. The government should fund demonstration projects aimed at reducing management alienation and disseminate information relative to project outcomes.

3. The government should encourage, through educational and public information programs, the growth of more realistic perspectives about the nature of work and careers and what they can and cannot do in affecting one's views and satisfactions on life.

Our position is that since the government provides a wide variety of financial supports for a veritable multitude of social ills, why should they not fund a program that deals with the multidimensional implications of the career success/personal failure syndrome? We are, of course, aware of the claimants to public funds in our society. We are not insensitive to many of these claims. However, we believe that the problems we are dealing with here are as serious as many others and require serious governmental interest. People involved in career success/personal failure crises are in pain. They are experiencing alcoholism, drug addiction, and family disintegration. The costs to society and to work organizations are great. These are heavy, damaging costs by whatever accounting system one uses, and it is frivolous to feel that, somehow, the problems are not as important because the people involved have higher-than-subsistence-level incomes.

There are two major ways that the government can provide financial assistance in this area. The first is to provide tax incentives to private-sector organizations that are willing to initiate programs aimed at dealing with this problem. Since this has proved to be an effective mechanism for stimulating entrepreneurial activities and for certain environmental problems, we suggest that providing tax incentives for midcareer development programs aimed at the resolution of the career success and personal failure crisis could be a highly effective tool. We fail to see any inherent problems here and we see manifold benefits.

The second approach the government can take, and one that is not antithetical but complementary to the above, is to fund programs directly, to evaluate them, and to disseminate their results. This can be done through appropriate grant and contract programs and through an encouragement of the development and evaluation of programs within government agencies themselves.

Government is by far the largest employer in our country, and our discussion is as applicable to high-level executives with government agencies as to those in the private sector.

In addition, we feel that the government can, through appropriate educational and public information programs, encourage a different perspective on the meaning of work, careers, and how they function in influencing our lives. We believe it important to learn how to make more rational choices in our work, to learn what work and career success can and cannot do in terms of our life satisfactions, and to develop a more realistic perspective on how our work careers should relate to the rest of our lives. It is our opinion that we have too long been in the grip of a naive belief that emphasizes a materialistically oriented success ethic. We have too long felt that status considerations and external values are outcomes that generate a satisfying life. The uncritical acceptance of this assumption has led to destructive outcomes for society, organizations, and individuals. We think this needs to be changed and that government, through its influence on educational and public information programs, has a crucial role to play in implementing this change.

SUMMARY

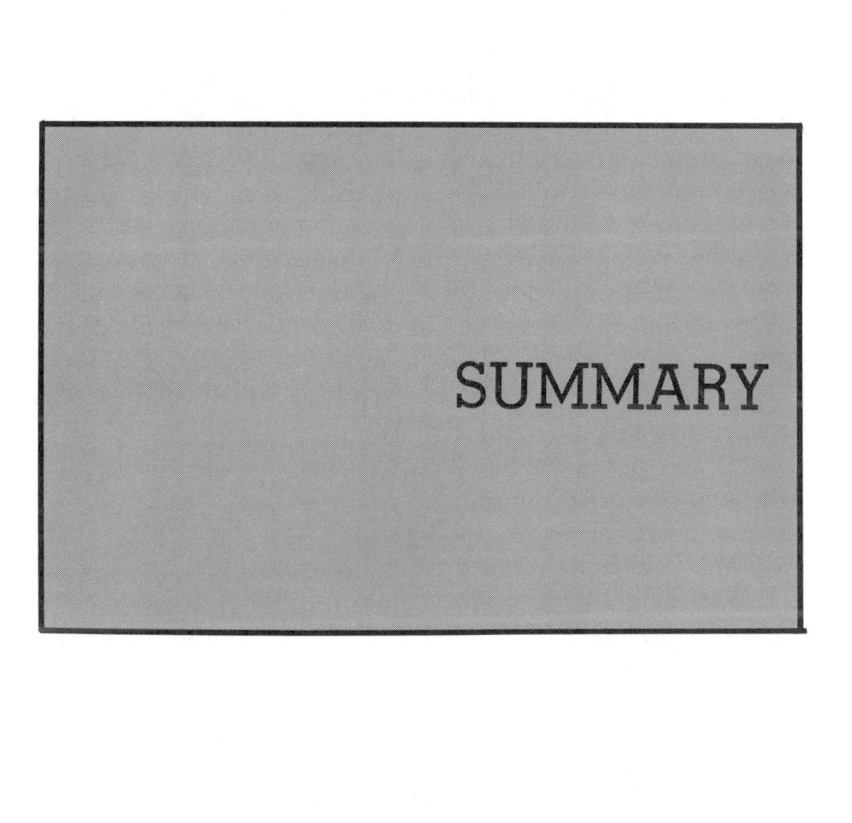

An increasing problem in our society is the growth of the personal failure syndrome among occupationally successful individuals. Often this manifests itself in personal and social alienation among managers in our work organizations.

Personal alienation reflects the degree to which the person feels there is a separation between his real being and his everyday activities. Such an estrangement generates an impoverishment of the individual's sense of self, with a consequent growth in self-destructiveness, the adoption of meaningless choices, and an apathetic noninvolvement in life.

Social alienation involves an estrangement from other people and groups, with a consequent lack of interactional effectiveness, a lack of concern for group goals, and, at the extreme, aggression and hostility toward others. Since the continued growth of personal and social alienation among managers has negative implications for our work organizations, the individuals who work in them, and the society of which they are all members, an understanding of the factors influencing the growth of this phenomenon is crucial. Efforts also need to be devoted to developing appropriate remedial interventions. This book has been concerned with both of these goals.

Two types of direct influence on the growth of management alienation have been proposed. The first of these consists of a set of psychological states resulting from life experience. These psychological states occur when the individual realizes the existence in his life of (1) *contradictory life demands*, (2) *disconfirmed expectancies*, (3) *a sense of external control*, and (4) *a loss of affiliative satisfactions.*

The second type of influence on management alienation is the developmental stage of the individual manager. More specifically, we propose that significant factors in the development of management alienation are the attitudinal, emotional, and cognitive characteristics associated with the midlife years. These characteristics include (1) the realization of one's aging, (2) the narrowing of choices, (3) the recognition of goals never to be achieved, and (4) changes in those individuals who constitute the manager's social context.

Given, then, the growth of alienation, personal and social, what happens? First, the alienated individual goes through a period of distress. Second, he reacts, sometimes positively, sometimes negatively. On the far-right column of Figure 1 we have outlined several types of reactions that can take place. What determines which will occur? These are a function of the factors listed in the column headed "environmental influences and interventions."

One possible change program we suggest is a restructuring of the manager's job when appropriate. A change of pace in one's daily activities can, in and of itself, lead to a new, more meaningful perspective on one's life, and sometimes people react positively to changes in daily work experience even when there does not seem to have been a major financial gain or growth in status. Just a change in everyday life can overcome the sense of alienation we have been referring to by giving a person an opportunity to utilize a different aspect of his capabilities. (We should note, however, that sometimes an unplanned change will only make things worse by adding the necessity of coping with a surprise to an already overburdened psychological system.)

A second set of factors influencing the possible reactions to alienation are change programs that can be undertaken by organizations, individuals, or societal/governmental institutions. We have focused on these change programs in Chapter 3. Among the programs discussed are (1) realistic job and career previews for all family members in order to reduce the number and degree of disconfirmed expectancies, (2) personal growth training programs such as assertiveness training and group training, (3) assessment centers aimed at accurate individual diagnostic evaluation counseling, and (4) career counseling programs for managers in their midlife stage.

As we indicate, these interventions can be initiated by individuals themselves, by single work organizations, or by societal institutions. Thus, while we focus mainly on what organizations can do in their own policies and practices, we also note that these problems can be dealt with on an individual and societal level as well. We particularly stress that this could be implemented best if we had societal structures and institutions that (1) value individuality and individuals, regardless of the

SUMMARY

nature and extent of their career achievement; (2) value and encourage choices involving change and redirection throughout life rather than just in the early 20s; and (3) provide sufficient economic and governmental supports to encourage meaningful change.

It is our belief that these patterns are beginning to emerge in our society, albeit slowly and with great resistance. Therefore, we should not be overly pessimistic. Obviously, some change is occurring and a new, more individualistic American life-style is evolving. Companies are taking an active role in managing their external environments, both alone and in conjunction with other companies and government agencies. Once they are convinced of their value, as is already occurring, we can expect to see an increasing number of realistic career previews, assessment centers, personal growth training programs, and so on, both within industry and government and in the nonwork world outside. Unfortunately, however, there are but a few realistic job preview programs today. Most assessment centers of a comprehensive nature, outside of specific organizations, and most personal growth programs are either (1) too general to be of great use to the manager, (2) too few in number, and (3) too gimmicky. We think this can and will be changed, but until it is, our opinion is that many of the good programs that will be developed in the foreseeable future will be corporation-specific.

Participation in personal, organizational, and societal change programs is only one way in which a particular manager may react to his sense of personal and/or social alienation. He may also, at this time, turn to his family for sustenance if he perceives the family as a group to turn to to reestablish his sense of self and his sense of relationship to others. The family *can* exert a positive supportive influence. However, if the affiliative ties are no longer there, as is often the case, the alienation continues to feed on itself. For many executives this turns out to be the case. During the years of climbing they have cut themselves off from wives and children, who, in turn, have cut themselves loose from the husband and father in their own quest for emotional survival. There is also the oppressed feeling many successful men have that their families see them essentially as mechanized tools who funnel in the money necessary for the consumeristic, high-status life-style they enjoy. The family's reaction to the alienation that occurs in a specific situation depends upon the individual manager and his family.

Above all of these influences on a particular person's reactions to his feelings of alienation, however, is whether he believes change is possible. Is the word a closed system to him? Does he see change as hopeless in the light of his own feelings of powerlessness in the world around him? Beliefs such as these can negate virtually any attempt at growth because they doom such strivings to failure before they are even fully formulated, no less tried. It is our belief that such a perspective is unnecessasily negative and unwarranted. We can get out of the dilemma into which we have put ourselves. We need only the willingness to try.

CASE STUDIES IN CAREER SUCCESS / PERSONAL FAILURE

JIM G.
CONTRADICTORY
ROLE DEMANDS

Jim G. arrived in Minneapolis in the late 1950s to attend the University of Minnesota. The son of a lawyer in a medium-sized South Dakota community, Jim's goal at the time was to attain his bachelor's degree at the university and then move on to graduate work in economics and finance at an institution such as Harvard or the University of Chicago. His eventual career goal was to move into the area of corporate finance and investment, preferably in Wall Street. Jim had relatives and family friends in the New York financial community and the possibilities of such a career had been introduced to him relatively early in life at family get-togethers.

His undergraduate years were satisfactory in several ways. He attained considerable academic success in his studies and he was also able to get involved in a number of local financial activities of a school and/or community nature. The late 1950s and early 1960s were a time of great growth in the Minneapolis-St. Paul area and the University of Minnesota had, in response, developed a continuing series of institutes, seminars, and conferences designed to help the growing local communities with their problems. It was with such activities that Jim was often involved during his undergraduate and also his graduate years.

In his senior year Jim met Karen H., a Minneapolis girl from a large, working-class family who was a commuter student at the college and also virtually self-supporting. Jim, who had grown up comfortable and secure in a small-town environment where his family was known and respected, was very much attracted to Karen's intelligence and drive. In fact, it was because of this attraction that Jim decided to stay at the University of Minnesota for his master's degree and to move on at a later date. During the next year and a half Jim and Karen became more deeply involved with each other and also with the growing number of community activities in Minneapolis. Money was being raised to bring a major repertory theatre to Minneapolis and to build a new hall for the Minnesota Symphony, by then a major American orchestra. Increasingly, the Twin City area was becoming more sophisticated and making available new and broader vistas for Jim and Karen, both of whom were more than eager to take advantage of them. In the meantime, Jim's graduate education progressed and almost without planning or forethought the day arrived when Jim found himself in possession of a brand new PhD. in finance, a position in a state agency dealing with the economic problems of northern Minnesota, and a wife. To add to his euphoria at the time, Jim's closest friend had completed his medical education in the East and had moved to Minneapolis to join the faculty at the medical school of the university.

Although life became increasingly pleasurable for Jim in Minnesota, he continued to talk of leaving the area for one of the major financial centers of the country. Continuing to spur his ambitions at this time were his cousins and friends in the New York Wall Street community whose connections and ability to provide assistance in this type of career had become even stronger.

Time passed and a son and daughter were born to Jim and Karen. The added responsibilities led Jim to view his state agency salary as no longer sufficient and Jim began his job-hopping years. Suburban communities, hungry for expertise, would hire him at a nice salary, but once the change was made, things never seemed to go as anticipated and Jim would move on again. Eventually, Jim moved into an attractive position with a Minneapolis-based company, bought a beautiful suburban home, and talked almost not at all of his earlier dream of a career in corporate financial management. Karen found a job in a local nursery school and became active in church and local community politics. Both were attractive, personable people and their social popularity increased over the years, both for themselves and because they could always be counted on to commit their time, energy, and considerable talents for any worthwhile cause.

All went well until Jim's forty-third birthday party. All their friends came, including Jim's still-close boyhood friend, now the head of a very prestigious unit at the Mayo Clinic and generally recognized as a major worldwide authority in his field. Few talked about it openly, but many people who knew his work believed that a Nobel prize might eventually be added to his rewards. Emptying ashtrays after the guests had gone home, Jim began to take stock and as he spoke, he increasingly did not like what he saw. He realized that he had been moved into a plateaued position in his company and he also saw why this had happened. Although he had always been available to coach Little League or serve on search committees for a new minister at the church and had never missed one of his daughter's dance recitals, his devotion to his job had not been on the same level. He had rarely been available to work after hours, had almost never taken on the special problems or projects that were constantly coming up, and he had traveled only rarely, and even then with a noticeable lack of enthusiasm. At each choice point, when Jim had had a choice to make betweeen the demands of the company and the demands of his family and/or his community interests, the company had almost always come last. Now he was 43, with a good family life, liked and respected in his community, but at a dead end in his career.

Those close to Jim found the next few years grim. Karen could not understand why a man with a good job (even if he was plateaued), a supportive family, and the friends they had could be so angry and so unhappy. Yet he was. Jim searched almost frantically for a new change in his career. He looked for opportunities to increase responsibilities and challenges in the job he had and he called friends and former graduate-school classmates, now scattered around the country. One change he considered very seriously was a move into academia, but professorships at the level he desired were not easy to come by in the 1970s for one who had not previously made his mark in his field. The best he could find was an assistant professorship at a small college at about one-fourth of his current income, a clearly unacceptable choice.

For the first time since they met the relationship between Jim and Karen became strained and conflict-ridden, with the tension between them reaching its apex when Jim was offered what seemed to be a good position with a small, but growing real estate firm in San Diego, California. The problem was that it involved giving up their home and the life they had cultivated for years in Minneapolis for a moderately risky move to an area neither knew much about or with which neither had any familial or friendship contacts. Yet, the opportunity did seem to be challenging, and part of Jim wanted very much to accept it. Karen, however, was adamant. She and the children would never consider such a move. To leave their friends and secure environment was unthinkable and, to punctuate her feelings, she accepted the principalship and a position on the board of directors of the nursery school to which she had devoted much energy on a part-time basis over the years.

Jim eventually made the decision to stay with his wife and children in Minneapolis, even though his job had not really proved very amenable to upgrading and had stayed about the same. The result has been that he now focuses even more on pleasures and interests that are non-job-related. He speaks with great pride about Karen's new position and how she was able to secure increased federal financing to turn a somewhat sleepy little nursery school into a growing, expanding day-care center and primary grade school. Each of his children's achievements now seem to assume monumental importance to him, and recently he has spent weekend after weekend poring over college catalogues and advising his son on the relative advantages and disadvantages of each school. However, Jim does not see the passive resistance of his son during these conversations and the fact that he, the father, is far more enthusiastic about the whole matter than is the son who will be attending the school eventually chosen. Nor does the father see the highly idiosyncratic and emotionally erratic behavior of his daughter. Instead, he focuses only on her dancing talent and her attractiveness. Karen, who is highly grateful for Jim's decision and who has no desire to reintroduce tension into the family, is perhaps more realistic about their children than her husband is but says little, hoping that things will work out for the best. In the meantime, Jim has become even more active in the community, heading a number of church activities, joining the library committee, and becoming more involved in overall school issues. Eventually, he will probably run for the school board, a major position in the commnity where they live. At home, when they have friends in, Jim will also frequently serve as chef, spending time concocting various sophisticated dishes with which to dazzle their guests.

Jim, confronted with the choice between career and home, chose the latter even though it probably meant the end of his career dreams and aspirations. As a result, he has had to give up part of himself and to focus on seeking satisfactions elsewhere. Our belief is that although this is sometimes an unavoidable problem, it frequently does not have to be if it is realized beforehand. This was not true here. Jim and Karen, bright and personable, nevertheless gave little thought to these matters and they drifted for years. Eventually, Jim's realization of his lost career generated a sense of personal alienation which threatened both himself and his family relationships. We do not pass judgment on how Jim and Karen eventually resolved the situation. However, we do suggest that had they had some foresight, the results would have been better for them, for Jim's career, and for the organization in which he works.

JACK L.
DISCONFIRMED EXPECTANCIES

Jack L. had been one of the toughest kids in one of the roughest areas of Los Angeles. A poor student in his elementary school days, he came under the influence of a very strong willed teacher when he entered high school. This teacher opened the world of achievement and occupational aspiration to him by exposing him to various "role models." These were people from Jim's background who had achieved considerable status and wealth. Frequently, also, Jack and the teacher would discuss the benefits of such wealth and status and how they could be achieved. Looking back now, it can be said that Jack's experiences with this teacher really laid the foundation for Jack's life and became the cornerstone upon which he built his career.

From that time of high school until the present, Jack's life has been marked by hard work and ambition. For him, college consisted of full-time evening employment in a restaurant after a regular schedule of classes at one of the more challenging local institutions. Upon graduation, Jack went to work in the restaurant industry on a managerial level, reasoning that (1) competition with the new graduates would be less since few people his age would be willing to work the evenings and weekends necessary and (2) the financial rewards would be great if he were successful. Although his assumptions, particularly the first, might have been questionable, his success was not. He did so well that within a few years Jack became a district manager for the corporation which owned, among its many subsidiaries, the restaurant he had worked in while attending college. His record as district manager was so outstanding that eventually he moved into a position with a large corporation which was one of his firm's major suppliers. This move was a sign to him that his ambition and willingness to work seven days a week, if need be, had paid off and would bring him even more rewards in the future if he continued this type of work and career commitment.

Jack's career with the new company was, therefore, similarly successful. Over a period of years Jack moved through a series of positions, each one higher than the last and each involving a geographic move for his family. Eventually, he moved into the position that had been his goal—executive vice-president of sales and marketing.

It was also as a result of this last promotion that Jack was able to build a very impressive home. Five houses and five communities after joining the company, Jack had his dream house. Set on a large lot in a beautiful area of town, the house was truly a showcase for the small city in which the corporate headquarters were located. Jack and the architect had worked side by side in its design and the result was an excellent example of good taste and attractiveness.

It was apparent, however, that Jack's interest in the house and his satisfaction with it were not shared by his wife or his children. Elizabeth, Jack's wife, had changed considerably from the withdrawn, rather traditional girl he had married before he began his corporate climb. A trained teacher, she complained bitterly about their frequent moves and had refused to take any part in planning or decorating their latest home. Perhaps even more significant, she was now showing a lack of interest in Jack's career and the problems he was facing at work. This was something new to Jack and a great loss to him since he had, during the course of their marriage, come to rely greatly on her calmness and on her stability of judgment. Now, when he needed her greatly as a result of some of the severe problems he was facing, she was refusing to help. Instead, she was withdrawing more and more from his particular needs and asserting herself more and more in ways that Jack found disconcerting. She talked of a career of her own and of developing a more independent life for herself. She was also showing a lack of interest in the problems their children were facing, a fact that Jack also found distressing and very surprising considering her great interest in their children during their growing years. Now, as they had attained young adulthood and were still having problems, his wife was withdrawing and leaving him to handle the situation.

Perhaps Jack would not be so upset if his job were not causing him difficulties. But this is not the case. There are several very difficult problems demanding his attention. One of these concerns the extramarital exploits of one of his key managers. Although Jack prides himself on keeping out of the personal lives of his employees, this particular manager is taking few precautions in his affairs and his activities are the talk of the plant. In addition, the man's wife has taken it upon herself to write letters to the company president detailing her anger and bitterness but at the same time insisting that her husband be kept on his job to protect her financial security. Jack, himself, is bothered by the matter on several grounds. First, he is perceptive enough to realize that he is threatened because his own marriage is having difficulties. Second, he believes strongly that a man's private life is his own affair. As long as a person does his job, it is not the business of the company to interfere. However, he sees that the man's activities are having a detrimental effect on his job performance, although he cannot prove it in an objective manner. Jack is feeling inordinately pressured because the company president has tossed the matter into his lap without any specific recommendation. Jack does not feel that this is fair.

Jack is also dealing with the possibility of a major sales and marketing reorganization. He has to determine whether certain product distribution patterns are overextended and whether the company should decrease the size of its marketing area for these goods. On the one hand, Jack feels that there is good reason to follow this approach because of the general weakness of some of their sales force and the fact that personnel could be shifted into more efficient working units in order to develop a stronger overall presence. However, Jack is also constantly being faced with the demands of the company president that sales volume be increased. He is also upset by the idea that some employees would be let go by the changes. Jack feels that he is being put into an impossible bind here also.

Until a few years ago, almost to the time of their most recent move, Jack had been able to talk to his wife about these matters. Now, however, she is angry most of the time. She complains bitterly about the fact that they are living in "his house" in a community to which "his job" has taken them. She talks continually about the loss of her own opportunities for growth and the fact that life holds nothing for her. Although Jack does not respond to these attacks, he believes she is being unfair. He feels that he has been a good husband and that his hard work over the years has been as much for her and for the children as for himself. They live in the house as much as he does and the overwhelming amount of his income is spent on them. He believes that he allows Elizabeth great discretion in running the household and that he makes few demands as to how the money should be spent. It is unfair, he feels, for his wife to complain in the late 1970s that he did not behave in the 1960s the way he would probably behave today if they were starting over again. He also feels that she bears at least part of the responsibility for the course of her life and that it is not fair for her to blame him for all her failures and disillusionments and not give him credit for the fine life he provides her.

Jack is also somewhat disillusioned as far as his children are concerned. His son, now 21, shows little interest in anything that promises career advancement. He is working as a cabdriver in Chicago and refuses to listen to his father's entreaties that he return to the college he left at 19. In fact, communication between Jack and his son is almost nonexistent at this point.

The situation is slightly better with his daughter, but there are problems here also. At 20, she has already been through one marriage and shows few signs of having learned much. She is an infantile person who looks to her father for guidance more than he believes she should. Although he is aware that he may have encouraged this dependency when she was younger, he feels that his wife is now partially to blame because of her increasing withdrawal and her anger toward him. He is trying to convince his daughter to return to school and may succeed.

CASE STUDIES IN CAREER SUCCESS/PERSONAL FAILURE

Increasingly, however, he wishes that Elizabeth would handle these family matters so that he could concentrate on his job problems. Recently, he has begun to think about his old interests in architecture and construction. Although he does not want to go back to school, he now finds himself daydreaming about opening a construction firm specializing in custom-built homes similar to his own. He realizes, however, that his material comforts are important to him and that he would have great difficulty in adjusting to the reduced income that would be involved in this type of job change.

It is our impression that the outcome of Jack's problems will be positive. He has been a coper and problem solver all his life and there is little reason to think that he will lose this ability, even though he now has problems he never expected during his climb upward.

More specifically, we think Jack will resolve his problems by reducing his workaholism and his fear of making a mistake. He will resolve the problems facing him on his job by accepting his own fallibility and by making decisions which will hurt some people but which will lead to positive outcomes overall. This may lead to the discharge of some personnel such as the least effective salesmen and the disciplining of the straying executive, but these are part of his responsibilities and he will accept them.

He will also come to grips with the fact he can help his children only so much and that they are responsible for their own lives. Similarly, he will reestablish his marriage because he wants to do so and because his wife, who has not left despite her anger, clearly wants him to do so. We do think, however, that Jack is going to need some help in dealing with his desire to make perfect decisions that do not antagonize people. Because Jack has an essentially realistic orientation toward life which will lead him to seek this help, we believe he will learn to deal reasonably effectively with the fact that the expectations he had of the benefits of career success were and are far greater than the reality often is.

FRANK R.
EXTERNAL CONTROL

Frank R. was born lucky. The son of an affluent, respected businessman, he now heads the company his father started thirty-five years ago. His tennis game is so outstanding that he is often invited to play with visiting professionals at the tennis club to which he belongs and his wife is, at 40, as attractive as when he married her twenty years ago.

Frank R.'s father, now in his early 70s, is one of the most prominent figures in the medium-sized Far Western community in which he has lived nearly all his life. This position comes partially from the dominance of his personality but even more so from the fact that he has been one of the most successful entrepreneurs in that area of the state. The most significant of his enterprises has been a chain of wholesale outlets in the housewares/home furnishing/home decorating business that he began prior to World War II and which became, by the mid-1960s, one of the largest of its type in the industry in terms of both gross sales and net income. It is generally agreed by those who know the situation that the major reason for this success in a hotly competitive industry was the ability, skill, and determination of Frank's father. A motivated, hard-driving man, he worked seven day weeks for years, supervising all aspects of his operation and becoming expert in all its problems. His particular specialty, however, was always sales. He is still highly involved in this end of the business and even now is constantly looking for new sales promotions and variations of existing product lines. Most important, he has built a personal customer following that has long been the envy of both his competitors and his friends. Among the techniques he used in building this reputation over the years was to invite his customers to his home where they would often play tennis with his growing son, Frank R.

Five years ago the growth of the chain and the opportunity to assure the financial future of his family for generations led Frank R.'s father to sell the business to a large conglomerate in a multi-million-dollar deal. Frank R. was involved in two ways. First, his father turned over half of the sale price to his son, thus making him a millionaire also. Second, he insisted that the terms of the sale include a ten-year contract for his son to serve as general manager. Although such clauses are quite common for the entrepreneurs themselves, they are unusual as far as third parties are concerned. Yet, Frank R.'s father was insistent and the buyer firm acquiesced because the company was so profitable.

Frank R. has now been general manager for five years. During his tenure, he has been confronted with a variety of problems, some of which he has recognized and attempted to deal with and some of which he has not.

As a result of corporate pressures, an increasing number of younger managers and executives with MBA-level training have joined the company. This has created a managerial force consisting of two very different types of managers: the new, younger people and the oldtimers who date back to preacquisition days. There is now conflict in the company as these mutually antagonistic groups work together. Open hostility at staff meetings and nasty backbiting are common. One illustration of the problem is that despite the fact that an expensive computer system has been introduced, it is not being utilized at maximum effectiveness because of the antipathy of the two groups toward each other. The old-line sales-marketing executives are unwilling to work with the young manager in charge of the electronic data processing facility. Throughout the company similar conflicts to these are taking place.

There are also legal and governmental pressures on company hiring practices, particularly as regards equal employment opportunity requirements. Until they were acquired, the company had been paternalistic. Personnel practices were typical of local community norms. Many members of the same family worked for the company and children often rose to positions higher than their parents had attained. Minority-group members were typically employed at lower occupational levels and were well treated according to the values of the time. However, none had ever been promoted above a first-line supervisory position and it was rare for them to climb even that high.

It was against this background that Frank R.'s appointment of a Mexican-American controller caused a sensation. "The old man wouldn't have done it" was an often-heard comment inside the plant and in the community at large. This reaction became even stronger when it became apparent that the new controller did not see himself as a token. Rather, with the support of Frank R. and corporate headquarters, he quickly instituted a set of financial controls and checks on management decisions which were far more stringent than those that had been typical in the past. While the younger managers were not greatly upset by the new procedures, the veteran managers, accustomed to the laxness of the old days, were upset and threatened by the new demands. Such radical changes in operating procedures would have caused difficulties under any circumstances, but the fact that they had been initiated by a minority-group member only made it worse. Although it was not overtly expressed, it was evident that the fact that the changes in accountability had been introduced and were now being enforced by a minority-group member was not favorably looked upon by the veterans in the company.

An additional continuing problem is Frank's father, the old entrepreneur. Although he is officially retired, he does not act that way. He is in the office three to four times a week. He frequently strides through the plant making comments of various kinds, just like in the old days. Often these comments take the form of administrative orders which he seems to expect to be attended to as though he were still in charge. He also feels free to

Case Studies in Career Success/Personal Failure

walk in on executive staff meetings and take an active, dominating role. This habit of his often comes across as demeaning to his son. A good illustration of this is a recent incident in which he broke into a meeting announcing that he had just convinced one of his customers to increase his standing order by 25%. He then proceeded to advise each member of the executive staff how the increase was to be handled, ignoring completely the agenda they had been working on prior to his entrance. During all of this his son sat quietly, not saying a word.

During his years as general manager, Frank R. has suffered a number of illnesses. Most severe has been a major heart attack which kept him out of commission for six months. In addition, he has suffered severe back pains which have defied diagnosis and continuing headaches. These aches and pains have, in fact, been so bad that he has started to cut down on some of his nonwork activities, including tennis. However, except for his recovery from his heart attack, he has remained greatly devoted to his work and has rarely missed a day. None of his friends nor his wife, either, has ever heard him complain or use physical illness as an excuse for avoiding his responsibilities.

Frank R. is one of the nicest, most intelligent, most likable people we know. He has had one serious problem, however, and that has been his failure to ask what he, himself, wants out of life. Having been born into a highly favorable situation, it seemed quite natural to move right in and assume his preordained role. Frank R. has always believed that there would be something wrong with him if he did not take advantage of the opportunities that have been provided for him. He has felt that it would be unfair to his father, who worked so hard for so many years to leave something to his family for his son to reject the business, and it would also be stupid. Yet, the person Frank has been most unfair to his father who worked so hard for so many years to minimized. By remaining in his father's shadow, he has continued to be an adolescent who has turned his anger and frustration in on himself rather than express it in open rebellion the way adolescents usually do.

Case Studies in Career Success/Personal Failure

Frank has built a shell around himself. It protects him from himself and enables him to meet his obligations as he sees them. One result has been that he, like his father, is also recognized as a highly respected member of the community. Yet, the cost to him has been tremendous. He is a person who is withdrawing more and more into a routine, almost robotlike existence. His marriage is now also suffering as his wife senses his remoteness and her dissatisfaction is causing him to withdraw even more. There are weeks in which no words more significant than his expected arrival time for dinner pass between them. More recently, a new problem has developed. While Frank remains at home trying to deal with his many corporate problems, his wife has begun to travel without him, sometimes accompanied by their younger daughter, sometimes alone.

Frank is, unhappily, a prime example of the career success/personal failure syndrome. A conscientious, concerned executive, Frank truly tries to do his job well. A responsible citizen, Frank meets the community norms for a man in his position. He is known for his civic spirit and support of charitable causes. A devoted husband and concerned father, Frank has never been known to be disloyal to his family in any way. To their friends and relatives, Frank and his wife seem to have an ideal, almost perfect marriage, free of conflict and filled with mutual care and concern. They are, without doubt, one of the politest married couples we know.

Yet within himself Frank R. is an almost completely alienated person. He is unable to confront his father and assume his role as the head of the company. His marriage has deteriorated to the surface relationship that appears to be so pleasant. It consists of two people moving so separately from each other that there are no areas for conflict or true engagement. He gets through each day in a robotlike fashion, meeting each of his obligations while he watches himself from inside, almost as if he were seeing a moving picture. Whatever midlife crisis has been brewing for Frank during the past few years seems to have been squelched and buried. Since his heart attack, Frank is even more the person he was before. We see no signs that Frank will change, except to become even more alienated from himself and emotionless as time goes on. Frank R. is illustrative of the fact that not all people make changes, even when troubled. Some choose to go on as before.

WILLIAM F.
LOSS OF AFFILIATIVE SATISFACTIONS

William F. was associated for twelve years with one of the major real estate investment firms in the Northeast. During that time he moved from an entry position into one of the major figures in the company, having been primarily responsible for a highly successful acquisition program in Mexico and Europe which helped turn what had been a moderate-sized firm into one of the major companies in the field. His salary grew so quickly during this time that the young MBA graduate who had found himself glad to be earning $12,000 a year when he first started out was, 12 years later, earning six figures a year, exclusive of bonuses and investment income.

This income and Will's status as a partner in the firm indicated clearly that he had, indeed, come a long way from his youth as the son of a clothing salesman of rather modest means. Will had grown up in a home where his mother spoke often of the need for a better life—a life of greater material goods, more fine antiques and artifacts, and more gracious living than the level she had had to accept as the wife of a man who could support his family but not provide for luxuries. She was a woman who had known some wealth as a girl before the onset of the Depression and she was determined that her sons, particularly her older child, would be the instruments by which she might regain her lost status. To this end, she would frequently impress upon them that they needed to go to the correct schools and to meet the kinds of people who would help them in later life and assure their future. To help in achieving this goal, she convinced her husband that they should live in a modest home in an affluent neighborhood so that the two boys would have an opportunity to meet rich friends and to go to good schools that would prepare them for top-notch colleges. Although it became apparent during these years that Will's relationship with his mother was a poor one which would only worsen over the years, Will did meet these goals. He made friends with those wealthier than he, did well at school and, eventually, after arranging for financial help, was accepted and enrolled at the Wharton School of the University of Pennsylvania.

At college Will's ambitions became even stronger and drove him even more. He attained an excellent academic record while working at a variety of part-time jobs, some more savory than others but all paying considerably better than most college student jobs. In fact, his income was so high that he was able to join a fraternity, a move that enabled him to become even more exposed to the people he wanted to meet. It was through the fraternity, also, that he met his first real girlfriend, Betty. Although her family was slightly better off than his in that they were able to pay her tuition, Betty had also found it necessary to work in order to have sufficient spending money. The relationship between the two quickly assumed an almost Pygmalion character. Will demanded that she wear only the finest clothing and nice jewelry and conduct herself, in general, like his image of a young debutante. His demands were great, but Betty seemed to be willing and able to meet them for a while. Eventually, however, the strain on her became too great and she told Will that she wanted out—that she would not be going to Boston with him when he enrolled at the Harvard Business School, to which he had been accepted.

Will's reaction to the loss of his girlfriend was not overwhelming. Although he had had some feeling for her and had liked the idea of having a girl around to take to fraternity parties and the like, Will's major energies were almost always directed at his work and career. Women, to him, were very pleasant but not the main focus of his life. With this attitude, it was lucky for

Will that he met Sally, a very attractive young woman from the upper-class background he admired so much. Will's ambition and motivation attracted her greatly. To her there was little doubt that he would go through the Harvard Business School with little difficulty. He would then move into the career in business he wanted so badly and would be highly successful at it. He seemed to her to be much more interesting and much more dedicated to his career than the boys she knew, most of whom seemed to be planning to enter their fathers' successful business or law practices.

A mutually attractive relationship developed, culminating in marriage and the setting up of housekeeping in Boston where Will attended Harvard and Sally taught in a local school before becoming pregnant. Sally was the perfect wife for Will. She demanded nothing from him except that he be ambitious, a demand he was all too happy to meet. She did not require any outlay from him. She knew how to dress, to furnish an apartment in good taste, and to prepare gourmet foods at a few minutes' notice. Also important for Will was that Sally had some independent funds inherited from her father which she was willing to have Will invest. Once she turned this money over to her husband, Will had the money he needed to begin his career, and begin it he did. Will's investments were so successful and well thought out that he attracted the attention of his wife's stepfather, a retired entrepreneur with money to invest and an interest in doing so. The two men hit it off well and a number of successful ventures were undertaken which were so mutually profitable that they are still held jointly by the two to this day, despite the changes in their relationship which will be detailed below.

Upon graduation Will joined a real estate investment firm and his ambitions, capabilities, and motivation now found appropriate expression. He worked 12 to 14 hours a day at the office and then worked at home. No notice was ever too short for him to take a client home to dinner, nor did Sally ever seem to complain. In fact, from the viewpoint of the office, she was the best of the young wives. She, alone, seemed to have been untouched by the women's liberation movement and she seemed to have no other interests except mothering, taking care of her home, and helping Will in every way that she could. She did not mind the dislocations involved in corporation climbing and bore them all with good humor. Perhaps an extreme example of her attitude, but a true illustration nevertheless, was the day she drove their two older children to her in-laws and then went to the hospital, while in active labor, to give birth to their third child, without bothering her husband at the office.

Within a decade after his entry into the firm, Will was a partner. He and Sally were now living in a beautiful home in a prestige suburb and had a live-in housekeeper to help care for the children. There were three cars in the garage, one a Mercedes. They skied at their condominium in Colorado, vacationed in Spain, and ate in New York's finest restaurants, usually with clients. Their children attended fine private schools, their after-school hours were filled with lessons of every conceivable nature, and their summer camp bills came to $6,000. They also belonged to a local country club where Sally played tennis and lunched nearly every day, but where Will was almost a stranger.

However, while their living conditions had changed, other aspects of their lives had not. Most specifically, Will's working hours had, if anything, increased. Although he rarely asked Sally to cook for clients anymore, his time with them was still great. He was gone three or four nights a week and was now going into the office every Sunday on a regular basis. As a result, he rarely saw his children, except on holidays, and was often absent from many of their activities. Although he and Sally quarreled about this, the quarrels were infrequent and, in fact, declined when Sally realized they were having little impact. However, the tension did affect their marriage and their relationship became increasingly strained.

Another source of estrangement was Will's relationship with his parents. Will's parents were delighted when Will married Sally and did everything they could to show her their pleasure. Sally felt their warmth and became a surrogate daughter to Will's mother, a relationship that became even closer when

CASE STUDIES IN CAREER SUCCESS/PERSONAL FAILURE

Will's brother married across racial and religious lines and opted for a life-style that did not meet his mother's maternalistic expectations.

When the children came, Will's mother became a doting and involved grandmother. Freed of the concerns for material advancement she had exhibited to her own children, she now let forth the emotions she had disciplined previously. The children adored her and she them. Will's father, too, having been deprived of close relationships with his own children because of long working hours and his wife's domination of their upbringing, became an actively involved grandfather. Sally encouraged these relationships and was herself a part of them. Will, on the other hand, increasingly deprecated his father, became alienated from and hostile to his mother, and grew angry at Sally for her own and the children's loyalty to his parents.

In one incident, the entire family was returning home from a restaurant when Sally requested that they stop at Will's parents' home to wish her father-in-law a happy birthday. This provoked a terrible fight, which ended with Sally and the children going into her in-law's house while Will sat outside in the car for over an hour.

Sally and Will might have drifted on like this permanently if Sally had not discovered a bill for some construction work of which she was unaware. Upon investigation she found that the construction bill was for a fireplace in a house that Will owned of which she was unaware and in which Will's secretary was living. The result was a series of confrontations between herself, Will, that eventually ended in a divorce. Will went to live with his secretary, who by this time was also the mother of a six-month-old child which he had fathered.

As a result of these events Will's estrangement from his parents and children by Sally has become almost complete. The children visit him on occasion but they do not get along with Will's secretary nor with Will himself. He has never known them very well, and with the tension of the divorce and the resultant bitterness, the relationships have gotten worse. In addition Will's behavior has so antagonized his father that he, his secretary, and his new child have been banned from his parents' home while Sally and her children remain on as good terms with them as previously.

Surprising as it may seem, however, Will's loss of relationships with his parents and children by his first marriage do not appear to have had much impact on him. During divorce negotiations with Sally he admitted to her that a divorce from his secretary, whom he had not even yet married, was a distinct possibility. Therefore, he could not blame Sally for pushing for as much money as she could get since he would probably have to pay a second settlement and alimony in the near future. He also seems to be withdrawing further from his children as the lingering guilt he felt at the time of the divorce dissipates.

Will has made some changes in his career. He has left the firm where he did so well and struck out on his own, a step that has meant a continuation of the long hours to which he has become accustomed. His income has remained high, although perhaps not so high as it was before, and this is somewhat of a problem since his expenses are now higher than ever since he is now supporting two households. He is also seeing a therapist twice a week. All of these expenses have served to motivate him to work even harder and to spend less and less time with his secretary and young baby. In this sense his day-to-day behavior seems to have changed little and there is little indication that Will has many regrets over the course of his life.

LARRY F.
MID-LIFE ALIENATION AND CHANGE

We first met Larry F. about eight years ago, prior to our interest in the career success/personal failure problem. He and his wife, Frances, and we, ourselves, were approaching our late 30s, years when we were all working hard in climbing the success ladder. For people like us, success meant job prestige, financial security, and a long-dreamed-of house in a beautiful suburb. These were Larry and Frances's goals and, to a great extent, they were attained.

One of the most important facts to know about Larry is that his parents were separated and eventually divorced when he was a boy. Such an event was not common in that time and place in New York City in the Italian-Catholic neighborhood where Larry grew up. Families there were noted for their closeness and family loyalties, and the shock to Larry, an only child, was great. He felt like a pariah when he compared his situation, just he and his mother, to the large, seemingly happy, extended families around him.

One result of this was that Larry developed an overwhelming need for friendship and social acceptance which remains a major component of his personality today. He often did favors for his neighbors and for the other boys on the block in the hope that they would invite him to share in their family get-togethers, and often they did. Larry was a pleasant, gregarious person, and he was a good person to enliven these parties.

Case Studies in Career Success/Personal Failure

Larry was an excellent student and a fine athlete, two attributes that enabled him to attain a scholarship to an elite private high school. Each day he left the neighborhood, boarded the subway, and emerged in a different work, a world to which he increasingly aspired and which led, eventually, to an excellent record and to the Columbia University School of Engineering.

There life repeated itself to a great extent. Larry was affable, easy-and-anxious to please, and a good student. Increasingly, however, Larry became estranged from the neighborhood in which he had grown up. He began to emulate his Columbia University classmates in both dress and speech, a process that led him increasingly to withdraw from the people he had known all his life. He now not only felt different from them, he also looked different and acted differently. As a result, he began spending more and more time at Columbia, bunking with schoolmates and returning to visit his mother only occasionally. Despite these changes Larry was not all that comfortable on future life. Morningside Heights, therefore, was his choice and different affected him there, also, but Larry knew the road to success in the world as he defined success. He knew that his friends at Columbia were more likely to lead him that way than were his old neighborhood friends. Also, if he felt a little out of place in both settings, and he did, it seemed only reasonable and intelligent to choose the setting that would help him most in his future life. Morningside Heights, therefore, was his choice, and toward the end of his junior year he moved into an apartment in the area with a group of friends.

The move was very significant for Larry in several ways. First, it was his final break with his past, an obviously important step. Second, he met his future wife when his roommate's sister came for a visit and brought a friend with her. The mutual attraction between Larry and Frances was great. She was a quiet girl, the oldest of five children of an affluent, suburban Irish-Catholic family which valued their social position, their wealth, and their material possessions. The contrast between her own withdrawn ways and Larry's liveliness, sense of humor, and good nature

CASE STUDIES IN CAREER SUCCESS/PERSONAL FAILURE

were very attractive to her and, despite her family's objections, they were married at the time of their mutual graduation from college.

Frances was confident at the time that with hard work she and Larry would be able to build a life that would match the success and pattern of her parents, a goal to which Larry agreed both implicitly and explicitly. They agreed they would both work to acquire a nest egg until Larry could handle the support of the family on his own. In both their minds there was the image of the beautiful home in the prestige suburb which would be furnished by an interior decorator and which would have a garage with a new car every two years and closets with beautiful, expensive clothing. Their dream, clearly, was "the good life."

Larry's career, until recently, met this dream. Attracted to the corporate world when he finished school, he worked in a number of positions over a period of years, moving up slowly but surely with each change. Despite this success, however, Larry never lost his fondness for socializing and for having a good time. Although he had been able to achieve some success in his managerial-corporate career, Larry was still more interested in being with people and having them like him. In fact, as the years went on, he began to show less interest in the technical demands of his work and began to rely more and more on his social skills in meeting his job requirements. The problem was that his social skills, considerable though they were, were not enough and Larry knew it. Yet, he continued to avoid the responsibilities and decisions that were part of his job, sliding from situation to situation. After all, he had much of what he wanted and what he had imagined corporate success to be like when he was a boy (i.e., the private office, the secretary, the executive privileges, etc.).

The situation could not remain this way permanently, and as Larry approached 40 an increasingly emotional dimension appeared in Larry's behavior. He found himself unwilling to make demands of his subordinates lest they dislike him and unwilling to undertake the effort and concentration required in order to meet the technical demands of his job. Instead, he focused on the superficial aspects and the comforts of his job, ignoring the demands that he needed to fulfill and which he avoided. Eventually, these attitudes started to have a serious impact on his performance and his supervisors began to count on him less and less. Larry realized this loss in the esteem in which he was held and his discomfort became even greater. He realized he was no longer doing a good job and might even lose the privileges which were really the only things he still liked about his work. Now that he was being faced with being plateaued into a job he no longer liked, his discontent festered even more.

Frances was now also becoming affected by the change in Larry and she was becoming resentful. Larry was going back on the shared goals they once had. She hadn't changed—why had he? And how were they going to continue to attain their goals if he was no longer interested in working hard and trying to get ahead? They had attained much but she wanted more and she thought he did also. But perhaps he did not? Frances now found herself just as discontented as her husband.

Although we are not certain how to define "midlife crises," the term, as it is generally understood, certainly seems descriptive of Larry and Frances's attitudes as they approached their 40s. The image of where they were going clearly seemed to be becoming inoperative. The plan for "the good life" was partially achieved but no longer motivating. They had keyed their life to the middle-class values and norms of the 50s and 60s, reinforced daily by contact with Frances's family. It was still their only guide. Yet, even though it had been achieved to a considerable extent, it had not brought them the satisfaction they wanted. Larry found himself more uninterested and more inadequate every day, a circular process that kept getting worse and worse. Frances, in the meantime, in the custom of the 1950s and 1960s, tried to keep up appearances to family and friends while feeling herself buckling under the strain.

Larry's not quite voluntary resignation from his job at this time was the straw that broke the camel's back. Larry and Frances were now faced with a new problem—money. The burden of providing some income fell on Frances, who fortunately was able to find a part-time job while the children were at school.

Case Studies in Career Success/Personal Failure

It did not pay much and it was quite menial for a woman who had worked for years as an executive secretary, but it was sufficient for Frances to keep up the appearances that were so important to her and to hold to the sham that she was working by choice rather than by necessity.

For a year Larry did not work at all. Nor did he look for another job. He seemed to be unable to decide what to do, alternating between periods of upswing and downturn. The upswings came when there were fewer money demands, when Frances was not under pressure from her family to do something about her life situation, and when Larry would agree that he bore reponsibility for his family and that he would eventually meet it. The downturns came when the situation reversed itself and when Larry would go into a highly depressed state and talk about a total withdrawal from his family and life situation.

Over a period of time, however, the upturns started to come more and more frequently and Larry talked increasingly about going into college teaching. He used as a model a friend who had built a career based on college teaching and consulting. Larry felt that this would be a desirable direction in which to go, since it would enable him to avoid the pressures of corporate life and also satisfy his needs for gregariousness and interpersonal contact with others. He began to look for a job at a university and because he had some knowledge of a particularly specialized area of engineering, he was able to find one. At the current time he seems to be doing well there and he is also trying to develop secondary sources of income through consulting activities, including the speechmaking he enjoys.

Larry appears to be satisfying himself at last. Although his college teaching income is considerably lower than his corporate income, Frances seems happier than she has been in a long time. Perhaps Larry's contentment is contagious. Perhaps they are laying to rest a set of images and a plan for life that was never truly suitable for them. Whatever the reasons, Larry and Frances may be coming to the end of their years of crisis. They seem to be reaching a new level of adjustment which is more satisfactory and meaningful than they have had in a long time. One of the reasons may be that Larry was able to effect the career change that many speak of but few attain and that he was able to do it in spite of the risks involved. It has been said that the essence of mental health is the willingness to take moderate risks, and this is what Larry did. He was fortunate in that he had a model available to him who illustrated a different life-style. Larry was able to see that there was an alternative to the life he was leading and the career he had been pursuing. Even more fortunate, Frances went along with him through his crisis period; she did not choose to end the marriage. With this support, tentative though it was at times, and with Larry's own ability to cope and his strength, which was probably the most important factor in the end, Larry's midlife crisis seems to be effectively resolving itself.

REFERENCES

1. Korman, A. K. *Industrial and Organizational Psychology.* Englewood Cliffs, N. J.: Prentice-Hall, Inc., 1971.
2. Campbell, A. Subjective measures of well-being. *American Psychologist,* 1976, *31,* 117–124.
3. Near, J. P., R. W. Rice, and R. G. Hunt. Work and extra-work correlates of life and job satisfaction. *Academy of Management Journal,* 1978, *21,* 248–264.
4. Henry, W. E. Conflict, age and the executive. *Business Topics,* 1961, *9* (21), 15–25.
5. Korman, A. K., and D. Lang. *Factors in career success and personal failure.* Paper presented at the Eastern Academy of Management, New York, Spring, 1978.
6. Tarnowieski, D. *The Changing Success Ethic.* New York: American Mangement Association (AMACOM), 1973.
7. Bartolemé, F. Executives as human beings. *Harvard Business Review,* 1972, *50,* 62–69.
8. Maccoby, M. *The Gamesman.* New York: Simon and Schuster, 1976.
9. Schultz, D. Managing the middle-aged manager. *Business Management,* 1974, *9,* 8–17.
10. Rabinowitz, S., and D. T. Hall. Organizational research in job involvement. *Psychological Bulletin,* 1977, *84,* 265–288.
11. Klein, K. L., and Y. Weiner. Interest congruency as a moderator of the relationship between job tenure and job satisfaction and mental health. *Journal of Vocational Behavior,* 1977, *10,* 92–98.

12. Cummings, T. G., and S. C. Manring. The relationship between worker alienation and work-related behavior. *Journal of Vocational Behavior*, 1977, *10*, 167–179.
13. Porter, L. W., and R. W. Steers. Organizational, work and personal factors in employee turnover and absenteeism. *Psychological Bulletin*, 1973, *80*, 151–176.
14. Korman, A. K. Organizational achievement, aggression and creativity: Some suggestions toward an integrated theory. *Organizational Behavior and Human Performance*, 1971, *6*, 593–613.
15. Seeman, M. On the personal consequences of alienation in work. *American Sociological Review*, 1967, *32*, 273–285.
16. Seeman, M. Alienation and engagement. In *The Human Meaning of Social Change*, ed. A. Campbell and P. E. Converse. New York: Russell Sage Foundation, 1972. 12:467–527.
17. Sennett, R., and J. Cobb. *The Hidden Injuries of Class*. New York: Alfred A. Knopf, Inc., 1972.
18. Chenoweth, L. *The American Dream of Success*. North Scituate, Mass.: Duxbury Press, 1974.
19. Bell, D. *The Cultural Contradictions of Capitalism*. New York: Basic Books, Inc., Publishers, 1975.
20. Albee, G. W. The Protestant ethic, sex and psychotherapy. *American Psychologist*, 1977, *32*, 150–161.
21. Cuddihy, J. M. *The Ordeal of Civility: Freud, Marx, Levi-Strauss and the Jewish Struggle with Modernity*. New York: Basic Books, Inc., Publishers, 1974.
22. Sarason, S. *Work, Aging and Social Change*. New York: The Free Press, 1977.
23. Milner, E. *The Failure of Success*, 2nd ed. St. Louis, Mo.: Warren H. Green, Inc., 1968.
24. Maslach, C. *Burn-Out: The Loss of Human Caring*. Berkeley, Calif.: University of California Department of Psychology, 1978. (Mimeograph.)

REFERENCES

25. Reisman, D. *The Lonely Crowd.* New Haven, Conn.: Yale University Press, 1950.
26. Slater, P. *The Pursuit of Loneliness.* Boston, Mass.: Beacon Press, Inc., 1970.
27. Korman, A. *Organizational Behavior*, rev. ed. Englewood Cliffs, N.J.: Prentice-Hall, Inc., 1977.
28. Novak, M. *In Praise of Cynicism (or) When the Saints Go Marching Out.* Bloomington, Ind.: The Poynter Center, Indiana University, 1975. (Mimeograph.)
29. Yablonsky, L. *Robopaths.* Baltimore, Md.: Penguin Books, Inc. 1972.
30. Gould, R. The phases of adult life: A study in developmental psychology. *American Journal of Psychiatry*, 1972, 5, 521–531.
31. Luft, J. *Group Processes: An Introduction to Group Dynamics.* Palo Alto, Calif.: National Press, 1963.

DATE DUE			
MAR 1 8 1984			
MAR 1 8 1984			

HF 5500.2 .K67

Korman, Abraham K., 1933-

Career success, personal failure